Nayef R.F. Al-Rodhan

The Three Pillars of *Sustainable National Security* in a Transnational World

The Three Pillars of *Sustainable National Security* in a Transnational World

Nayef R.F. Al-Rodhan

LIT

Cover Picture:
Blue Marble: Next Generation, NASA's Earth Observatory
http://earthobservatory.nasa.gov/Newsroom/BlueMarble/

Bibliographic information published by the Deutsche Nationalbibliothek
The Deutsche Nationalbibliothek lists this publication in the Deutsche Nationalbibliografie; detailed bibliographic data are available in the Internet at http://dnb.d-nb.de.

ISBN 978-3-03735-237-3 (Switzerland)
ISBN 978-3-8258-1067-2 (Germany)

A catalogue record for this book is available from the British Library

Dufourstr. 31
CH-8008 Zürich
Tel. +41 (0) 44-251 75 05
Fax +41 (0) 44-251 75 06
e-Mail: zuerich@lit-verlag.ch
http://www.lit-verlag.ch

LIT VERLAG Dr. W. Hopf
Berlin 2008
Auslieferung/Verlagskontakt:
Fresnostr. 2
D-48159 Münster
Tel. +49 (0)251–62 03 20
Fax +49 (0)251–23 19 72
e-Mail: lit@lit-verlag.de
http://www.lit-verlag.de

Auslieferung:
Schweiz/Österreich: Medienlogistik Pichler-ÖBZ GmbH & Co KG
IZ-NÖ, Süd, Straße 1, Objekt 34, A-2355 Wiener Neudorf
Tel. +43 (0) 2236/63 535 - 290, Fax +43 (0) 2236/63 535 - 243, e-Mail: mlo@medien-logistik.at
Deutschland: LIT Verlag Fresnostr. 2, D-48159 Münster
Tel. +49 (0) 2 51/620 32 - 22, Fax +49 (0) 2 51/922 60 99, e-Mail: vertrieb@lit-verlag.de

Distributed in the UK by: Global Book Marketing, 99B Wallis Rd, London, E9 5LN
Phone: +44 (0) 20 8533 5800 – Fax: +44 (0) 1600 775 663
http://www.centralbooks.co.uk/acatalog/search.html

Distributed in North America by:

Transaction Publishers
New Brunswick (U.S.A.) and London (U.K.)

Transaction Publishers
Rutgers University
35 Berrue Circle
Piscataway, NJ 08854

Phone: +1 (732) 445 - 2280
Fax: + 1 (732) 445 - 3138
for orders (U. S. only):
toll free (888) 999 - 6778
e-mail:
orders@transactionspub.com

Contents

ACKNOWLEDGEMENTS

This book was written in collaboration with **Sara Kuepfer** from the Programme on the Geopolitical Implications of Globalisation and Transnational Security at the Geneva Centre for Security Policy.

I am very grateful to **Dr. Bates Gill**, Director of the Stockholm International Peace Research Institute (SIPRI) (Stockholm, Sweden); **Professor James K. Wither**, Professor of National Security Studies, College of International and Security Studies at the George C. Marshall European Center for Security Studies (Garmisch-Partenkirchen, Germany); **Ambassador Dr. Theodor Winkler**, Director of the Geneva Centre for the Democratic Control of Armed Forces (DCAF) (Geneva, Switzerland); **Ambassador Dr. Fred Tanner**, Director of the Geneva Centre for Security Policy (Geneva, Switzerland); and **Dr. Graeme P. Herd**, Faculty Member, Geneva Centre for Security Policy (Geneva, Switzerland) and Associate Fellow, International Security Programme, Chatham House, London, for their constructive and insightful comments on the manuscript.

I would also like to thank **Bethany Reichenmiller** for her invaluable role in coordinating the production of this manuscript.

Finally, the author would like to express his special thanks to the faculty and staff of the Geneva Centre for Security Policy for their continued support.

CHAPTER 1

THE CONCEPT OF NATIONAL SECURITY

The 21st century requires radically new thinking about national security. States have become increasingly interdependent and today face a multiplicity of threats from many different sources, not just other states. Moreover, the information age is posing a new set of challenges to security establishments around the world. Intelligence agencies no longer have to worry about too little information, but about too much. They have to try to make sense of the plethora of information available, distinguish the relevant from the irrelevant and the true from the false, and coordinate and share information with the appropriate government agencies. This all has to happen in real time. National security councils and other security decision-making bodies are no longer endowed with the "luxury" of having 13 days to deliberate and weigh their options during a state of national emergency, as John F. Kennedy and his staff had during the Cuban Missile Crisis.

In past centuries, empires and states have come up with a variety of doctrines and strategies to protect their homeland from threats – which were, until recently, perceived as mostly state-based. After World War II, the United States (US) saw a need to coordinate security-related information and policy better among its different government departments and agencies. As a result, the United States was the first country to create a National Security Council, an institution tasked with assessing security threats and spotting emerging strategic challenges early; advising the executive on national security policy; and drafting strategy papers. The US model of creating a unified institutionalised setting within the government to deal with security policy and strategy has been adopted by several nations since. This study argues that a national security council or an equivalent institution in the 21st century is no longer just a "useful" addition, but an essential component of any state's ability to provide security for its people.

This book takes a fresh look at national security – past, present and future. The remainder of this chapter briefly discusses the concept of and main approaches to national security. Chapter 2 puts the different security doctrines embraced by European powers and the United States in historical context, pointing out how national security doctrines have evolved with changing international circumstances and experiences during times of war and peace. Chapter 3 describes how some states organise their national security today. The chapter focuses particularly on states with a national security council, a type of institution that is extremely useful for governments when dealing with the complexity of today's security threats. Chapter 4 identifies the nature and extent of the security threats that states face today, ranging from infectious diseases and state failure to transnational organised crime. It sets the stage for creating a new national security framework that takes account of the diverse threats in a comprehensive way. Chapter 5 puts forward a new approach to security and international relations in today's instant and interdependent world, drawing on emerging concepts in international security studies. Chapter 6 describes how an ideal national security council in the 21st century would look, taking into account the new circumstances of today's security environment. It puts forward a proposal for a new national security framework which builds on an innovative understanding of international relations and security in the 21st century.

1. Defining National Security

The concept of *security* is highly complex. Individuals and states may define it in different ways at different points in time. What all concepts of security have in common, however, is that "they are based on fear of actual and potential attacks on public authorities, persons and property".[1]

To a certain degree, security has objectively definable physical aspects – such as whether a country's borders are safe from attack and whether a state is able to guarantee a reasonable degree of law and order so that citizens can live free from physical harm. At the same time, there is also a more subjective dimension to the notion of security – the degree to which people perceive themselves to be secure from harm.[2] For instance, was the US population safer on 10 September 2001 than it was on 12 September 2001? Probably not, but the vast majority of US citizens probably "felt" safer before the realisation that terrorists could strike at any time and cause widespread havoc and suffering. Political scientist Arnold Wolfers gave expression to the ambiguity of the security concept by stating "Security, in an objective sense, measures the absence of threats to acquired values, in a subjective sense, the absence of fear that such values will be attacked".[3]

The modern concept of *national security* is inextricably linked to the emergence of the nation state. National security policy can broadly be defined as "a framework for describing how a country provides security for the state and its citizens".[4] The framework identifies and addresses both internal and external security threats and "seeks to integrate and coordinate the contributions of national security actors in response to the interests and threats deemed most important".[5]

Graham Allison points out that the size and relative power of each state determines how independent a state is in pursuing its national objectives. For instance, some European states have voluntarily given up sovereignty over their currency and now defer to the European Central Bank as a way of enhancing their objective of increasing national and common prosperity. Moreover, to preserve their territorial integrity and protect themselves from outside attack, small and weak states often form alliances or accept protection from a stronger power, thus voluntarily giving up some of their freedom of action to advance their national security objectives.[6]

The national security concept of a country is strongly influenced by the country's unique particularities – most importantly, the country's historical experiences. For instance, a country that has been traumatised by repeated attacks from neighbouring states laying claim to its territory will have a different approach to national security to a country that has never been attacked. Moreover, a country's geographical characteristics and its natural resources also influence national security thinking. For example, a state that is landlocked will have different national security needs to a state with a long coastline, and a country with no oil and gas resources will consider energy security a higher priority on its list of national security concerns than a state that is partly self-sufficient when it comes to meeting its energy needs.

2. An Evolving Concept

Traditionally, states have made a clear distinction between internal and external security. Already in the 16th century, the Italian diplomat and philosopher Niccolo Machiavelli distinguished internal threats to a ruler, which came from domestic attempts at subversion or internal rebellion, from external threats posed by hostile foreign powers.[7] This distinction is still reflected in the security apparatus of states today.[8]

Since the end of the Cold War, however, the distinction between internal and external security has become increasingly blurred. At the same time, the definition of what constitutes a security threat to a state has been broadened. Growing global economic interdependence, dynamic cross-border migration patterns, the multiplicity of transnational interactions and the rapid, global dissemination of information through new global communications technology such as the Internet make it much more difficult for states to maintain a sharp distinction between internal and external security challenges.

Moreover, states, particularly in the developed world, are no longer primarily concerned about so-called traditional security threats. Today, most developed states are not so much concerned about a conventional military conquest because their neighbours do not harbour any territorial ambitions. It is arguable, however, that this may only be a temporary condition, and national survival might well again become a priority security concern for states. With regard to internal security, most governments in the industrialised world are secure because most citizens inside these countries accept their government as legitimate. In particular, most liberal democracies face few internal or external political and ideological challenges to their system of government. Most developed states have democratically elected governments, and democracies purportedly do not wage war against each other.[9] Thus, in the case of most developed states, "territorial integrity and political autonomy", the very basis of state sovereignty, is not in jeopardy.[10] Current state borders – at least in the developed world – enjoy broadly based international legitimacy, and international law explicitly outlaws territorial conquest.

Clearly, the external conditions of states have changed, and so has their concept of national security. As Vincent Ferraro explains, the threat of terrorism, which currently dominates the security discourse in the United States, does not pose a traditional threat to the territorial integrity of states, nor are terrorists in a strong enough position to take over governments in the developed world. Instead, the terrorist attacks of 11 September 2001 on the US cities of New York and Washington, DC, did something else. Ferraro writes "What these attacks did appear to threaten was the quality of life of American citizens: most specifically, the ability of Americans to live free of fear".[11]

Hence, "traditional" security threats have given way to a series of "non-traditional" threats that have been given increased prominence in the past two decades. Among them are, for example, human-induced environmental threats, infectious diseases, large migration flows, state instability and international organised crime. Certainly, this is not to suggest that such non-traditional threats have not existed in the past. For millennia, human beings have died from environmental catastrophes and contagious diseases, as well as other threats that did not involve foreign armies or domestic armed rebellion. However, these so-called non-traditional threats have received increased prominence in the security discourse, partly due to the relative decline of more traditional military threats to states. In other words, they have become "securitised", that is, identified as threats to human, national and international security on a par with more traditional national security concerns. These security issues have also become more threatening to the dominant states in the system – the wealthy, developed West – which is another reason why they have gained increased prominence in the international security discourse.

What is more, non-traditional threats to states have acquired increased urgency in recent years because some of these threats have become more severe in the past few decades (e.g., as a result of rapid population growth and unprecedented levels of environmental degradation), and partly because of the growing interconnectedness and interdependence of states as a result of globalisation. Hence, a threat to one country can spill over to other countries much faster and more easily than before. Moreover, states have come to understand that other states are no longer the only relevant actors in international politics. Instead, states have started to recognise that "non-state actors" can be both "threats and partners".[12]

Taking into account the new context in which government officials operate, Richard Ullman broadened the definition of national security. He defined a threat to national security as "an action or sequence of events that (1) threatens drastically and over a relatively brief span of time to degrade the quality of life for the inhabitants of a state, or (2) threatens significantly to narrow the range of policy choices available to the government of a state or to private, nongovernmental entities (persons, groups, corporations) within the state".[13]

The US "Commission on America's National Interests" also reflects this evolution of the concept. Following World War II, the Commission defined the goal of the US national security strategy as "to preserve the US as a free nation with our fundamental institutions and values intact".[14] Today's version of the document formulates the same goal as "to safeguard and enhance the well being of Americans in a free and secure nation" – thus adding prosperity as a primary national security objective.[15] The dilemma that governments now face is that by defining national security too narrowly, that is, just in terms of hard-power threats from other states, they miss other significant threats to state security. By defining security too broadly, however, states run the risk of watering down the concept while failing to distinguish between threats that jeopardise their very existence and those that "merely" compromise the quality of life of their citizens.

3. Interests versus Issues

The multiplicity of definitions of national security and of ideas about how to prioritise and deal with different types of threats can all be grouped into two broad categories. Stephen Cambone suggests that we distinguish between two main approaches to national security policy making: one based on issues and the other based on interests. As the term suggests, the issues-based view focuses on the issues that cause security threats to states. This approach thus maintains that national security is inextricably linked to international security. By improving the quality of life of the world's population as a whole, there would be fewer conflicts and less suffering in the world and, consequently, fewer threats to the security of states.[16]

Furthermore, the issues-based approach stresses the need for countries to confront security threats together and encourages multilateral actions in conformity with international law and norms. According to this view, the particular interests of an individual state sometimes have to be subordinated for the greater good of the international community. According to Cambone, "issues" advocates usually put socio-political issues, such as human rights or transnational crime; economic issues, including economic sources of conflict; and military-strategic issues, such as the proliferation of weapons of mass destruction (WMD) and terrorism at the top of the national security agenda.[17]

The interests-based approach is much more state-centric, in the sense that the national interest and the security of one's state and citizens trump any other obligation – legal or otherwise – the state may have towards the international community. In the example of WMD proliferation, Cambone explains, the interests-based approach would primarily be concerned about "preventing, deterring, and reducing the threat of a WMD attack" on one's own state. Only after this "vital interest" has been met, this view would maintain, should a state become involved in helping to prevent, deter and reduce WMD use in the rest of the world (which the interests-based view considers an "extremely important" but not a "vital" interest).[18] Issues such as international human rights and environmental protection would, in this view, be classified as "important" because massive human rights violations abroad and environmental degradation would have major negative consequences for one's own state, but these threats would definitely have a lower priority than those national interests classified as "vital" or "extremely important" for the survival of the state and the safety of its citizens.[19]

In short, advocates of this approach focus on geopolitical and geo-economic issues and thus look for ways in which "competition among states can be prevented, managed, or successfully conducted".[20] In contrast, those who concentrate on global rather than national security (the issues-based view) want their state to be much more active in promoting international cooperation and collective action to tackle common threats. While identifying some of the same security issues, the two approaches prioritise these security issues differently.

The national security structures of states today are forged to support the interests-based approach rather than an issues-based security policy. Especially in democracies, it can be difficult for policy makers to convince voters and taxpayers that a particular issue – be it a humanitarian crisis or a failed state in a far-flung corner of the world – will directly affect the security of their nation if the issue is not addressed immediately. Writing in 1995, Cambone wonders whether taxpayers are willing to support the spending of resources and perhaps even the sending of troops to address a crisis that does not – and may never – directly affect the security of their own state.[21] Yet, in the case of the United States, the terrorist attacks of 11 September 2001 have to a certain extent shifted public perception regarding the origins of national security threats. The attacks demonstrated to many US citizens that failed states, poverty, local conflicts, real or perceived injustices and the spread of extremist ideologies far away from their nation's shore can indirectly lead to deadly attacks on their own territory. In other words, events that seem not to have anything to do with a state's national security may come to haunt the state later on. Such are the national security consequences of an instant and interconnected world.

While national security policies today are still dominated by an interests-based approach, the 21st century security environment is increasingly forcing states to think globally and multilaterally – thus becoming more issues-centred. Chapter 2 considers the way the national security doctrines of some of the key players in international politics have evolved over time.

CHAPTER 2

DIFFERENT STATE SECURITY DOCTRINES: A LOOK AT HISTORY

Although the concept of national security implies the existence of a nation state, societies since the beginning of human history have taken measures to protect themselves, be it through the manufacture of weapons or later the creation of formal military units. Besides maintaining a strong army, the Ancient Roman Empire, for instance, additionally sought to protect its territory by building a system of strong fortifications, the *limes*, around the edges of the empire to shield it from "barbarian" intrusions. Similarly, China made several attempts between the 5th century BC and the 16th century to build a wall on its northern frontier to keep foreign invaders out of the empire. The result of these efforts undertaken by several Chinese dynasties is a 6,400-km long wall, the largest human construction ever built.[22] This chapter examines the different national security concepts that have evolved in Europe, the United States, Japan and China over the centuries in the context of changing international circumstances.

1. Security Concepts in Europe

Europe is the birthplace of the modern state system. Once sovereign states started to form, they developed various strategies and doctrines to safeguard their territorial integrity and national sovereignty. Historically, European security concepts have been strongly based on calculations of power. Only after World War II, and especially since the end of the Cold War, have European states started to adopt a more comprehensive view of security.

(a) The Peace of Westphalia and the Creation of the Modern State System

During the Middle Ages, Central Europe was dominated by the Holy Roman Empire, a confederation of mainly Germanic territories ruled by individual noblemen and held together by their common allegiance to the Holy Roman Emperor and the Pope. Emperors saw their mission on earth as fulfilling the will of God, which took precedence over doing what was best for the welfare of the secular state. Although religion sometimes only served as a pretext for wars fought for dynastic and state interests, the concept of the nation state as a sovereign entity with fixed borders did not yet exist. At least in theory, the state during the Middle Ages was an instrument to serve religious purposes.[23]

The Reformation in the 16th century and the subsequent adoption of Protestantism by some of Europe's kings and noblemen destroyed the spiritual unity among the different European territories. The Thirty Years War in Europe, a war fought between the armies of the Catholic Holy Roman Empire and Protestant princes challenging the authority of the Holy Roman Emperor, brought no clear victor to the fore. Instead, the war ended with the conclusion of the Peace of Westphalia in 1648, which laid the foundation of the modern state system. The peace agreement was based on the principle of *cuius regio, eius religio* – which meant that each king or prince had the authority to determine the religion of the people living in his territory. As a consequence, there was no longer an overarching authority – the Catholic church was personified by the pope (spiritual affairs) and the Holy Roman Emperor (secular affairs) who had previously held the disparate territorial entities together. The states were now on their own. Each monarch was given the authority to rule over the people in his or her territory without outside interference; the principle of state sovereignty was thereby enshrined in the Westphalian treaty and recognised by its European signatories.[24] As John Elliott puts it, Europe after the signing of the Treaty of Westphalia "was to be a continent in which the secular interests of states were to be of more importance in the conduct of international affairs than their religious differences".[25] Important changes also occurred at the domestic level of European states, as they became increasingly consolidated and centralised. National armies were created, and states had to devise more efficient systems of taxation to pay for the military and the centralised bureaucracy.

Following the foundation of the modern state system based on the principle of state sovereignty, scholars and policy makers in Europe developed a series of theories to describe the nature of the state system. Moreover, statesmen started to devise doctrines and strategies to defend the sovereignty of their state vis-à-vis others and enhance the well-being and safety of their citizens. Some of these are examined below.

(b) The Emergence of Political Realism

The theoretical underpinning of the modern national security concept was provided by political realism.[26] Political realism is a theory that seeks to describe or prescribe relations between states. According to one definition, the theory "takes as its assumption that power is (or ought to be) the primary end of political action. . . . [Political realism is] either a prescription of what ought to be the case, that is, nations and politicians ought to pursue power or their own interests, or as a description of the ruling state of affairs – that nations and politicians only pursue (and perhaps only can pursue) power or self-interest".[27] Political realism is based on the premise that states are in perpetual conflict with one other. In an anarchic world, where there is no overarching authority that regulates state behaviour, a state has no other option but to look after itself and rely on its own capabilities to secure its existence. According to political realists, the need for self-preservation and the maximisation of power is therefore the motivating force that drives state action.

An early statement of this view can be found in the works of the ancient Greek historian Thucydides, who wrote about the war between Sparta and Athens in his book *History of the Peloponnesian War* in the 5th century BC. During the war, Athens threatened the Melians that it would invade and destroy their island if they did not join Athens in the war. The Melians, however, insisted on their right to neutrality and argued that showing mercy towards Melos would be in the long-term interests of the Athenians. However, Athens refused to take account of any arguments of justice put forward by the Melians, noting that Athens' military superiority would inevitably lead to the conquest of the militarily inferior Melians. In Thucydides' account, the Athenians thus famously concluded: "The strong do what they can and the weak suffer what they must".[28] Thucydides thereby implied that the conquest of the weak by the strong was an inevitable natural law that could not be modified – a fact of life that every statesman would have to accept and prepare his state for accordingly.

Niccolo Machiavelli, writing in the 16th century, came to a similar conclusion. He lived through a tumultuous era in early Renaissance Italy, where papal armies and wealthy city states in Italy were falling victim to invading foreign armies from France, Spain and the Holy Roman Empire. Alliances between states were constantly shifting, and governments were toppled or changed hands on a regular basis. Writing in this environment of constant insecurity and uncertainty, Machiavelli concluded that each state can only rely on itself and is required to do what is necessary to ensure its survival, even if this entails territorial conquest and the use of force.[29]

In the 17th century, the English philosopher Thomas Hobbes argued in his work *Leviathan* (1651) that as long as there is no common authority to which humans can submit and that regulates their interactions, there will be a state of perpetual war of all against all.[30] He wrote that humans, by their very nature, have a "general inclination" towards "a perpetual and restless desire of power after power, that ceaseth only in death".[31] Only an all-powerful government – what Hobbes refers to as a Leviathan – that is able to protect individuals from each other and from foreign invaders can restrain this basic human drive to maximize power at the expense of others, and hence allow them to channel their efforts towards more productive ends.[32] Ultimately, Hobbes implied, it is in the inherent interest of humans to live in peace by voluntarily submitting to a higher authority through entering into a social contract.

Political realism applies Hobbes' description of the state of nature to explain the relations between states in an anarchical world: without a world government, states are left to fend for themselves and pursue their security interests unrestrained.

(c) *Raison d'Etat*

The concept of *Raison d'Etat*, translated as national interest, describes the notion that a statesman has to do whatever is necessary to further the well-being of the state – be it in the military, economic or cultural spheres. The first country to advocate this policy was France, which was also one of the first nation states in Europe. The person who shaped the policy was Cardinal de Richelieu, First Minister of France from 1624 to 1642.[33] The concept was highly revolutionary at the time and signified a break from the old order based on religion and universal values, where wars were justified on religious grounds. During the Thirty Years War, France, a Catholic country, broke with the religious imperative of fighting on the side of Catholic countries and instead sided with the Protestants to prevent the Holy Roman Empire from dominating the continent. As a statesman, Richelieu drew a clear line between his private religious beliefs and state affairs, which he dealt with in purely secular terms. The idea that wars could be fought simply to pursue the interests of a state was truly revolutionary at the time. By putting the interest of the nation state above any other values, Richelieu laid the ideological foundations of the modern state.[34]

(d) Universality and Napoleon I

Following the French Revolution, which replaced the French monarchy with a Republic, France started to pursue a foreign policy based on universal ideals. Under Napoleon I, French armies conquered European territories and imposed republican ideals of liberty, equality and fraternity on the newly occupied territories. Napoleon thereby exploited the revolutionary mood in many European countries and subsequently crowned himself emperor, transforming what had been a revolution into a traditional bid for French supremacy in Europe. Napoleon believed that the best way to safeguard not just the integrity of French territory, but also its new domestic political order was to spread the same values among its neighbouring states and beyond. Doing so would not just strengthen the French Republican system domestically, but also greatly enhance France's position in Europe by providing ideological leadership and creating a European commonwealth led by France.[35] Only Russia and Great Britain were ultimately able to prevent French dominance on the continent. Napoleon's approach to national security was revolutionary because of its preoccupation with the nature of the domestic political system in surrounding states. By having the rest of Europe share the same political ideology and values, Napoleon sought to strengthen France's dominant position in Europe and the country's national security.

(e) Balance of Power and Splendid Isolation

In the 19th century, Great Britain developed a national security strategy that avoided entangling alliances and allowed it maximum flexibility and freedom of action. British leaders were convinced that the country could rest secure as long as no single power dominated the European Continent. In other words, its security depended on maintaining a balance of power in Europe. Hence, Britain would intervene on the continent only to prevent a strong power from dominating the continent by backing the weaker, countervailing power. As the British Prime Minister, Viscount Palmerston, once put it, "We have no eternal allies and no permanent enemies".[36]

The only guiding principle for British security policy was its national interest. As Palmerston explained in 1856: "When people ask me…for what is called a policy, the only answer is that we mean to do what may seem to be best, upon each occasion as it arises, making the Interests of Our Country one's guiding principle".[37] A few decades later, Foreign Secretary Sir Edward Grey stated: "British Foreign Ministers have been guided by what seemed to them to be the immediate interest of this country, without making elaborate calculations for the future".[38] Britain thus made its security decisions ad hoc as threats arose, doing what leaders felt was "best" for the country. According to Palmerston: "Our interests are eternal, and those interests it is our duty to follow".[39]

(f) The Concert of Europe

Following the defeat of Napoleon, representatives of the main European powers met at the Congress of Vienna in 1814-1815 to draw up a post-war settlement. Some historians have praised the settlement that came out of the Congress as laying the foundations for almost 100 years of relative peace in Europe. At the Congress, Great Britain called for an arrangement that could effectively prevent any European power from seeking continental hegemony in order to help keep each other's potential unilateralist ambitions, as well as France, in check. Consequently, the Congress established the Concert of Europe, a series of meetings between Europe's four great powers – Britain, Austria, Russia and Prussia – to settle disagreements peacefully and promote stability on the continent. Britain at the time insisted that France also be included to quell French resentment and to counterbalance the other four powers. France was able to join the Concert a few years later.

Although three powers – Russia, Prussia and Austria – also shared the fear of attempts at hegemony, their even greater concern was internal revolution. The three powers thus created the Holy Alliance, an arrangement by which the conservative monarchies agreed to support each other in fighting revolution. The Holy Alliance thus complemented the Concert of Europe through its commitment to maintain the domestic status quo in Europe.[40]

According to Kissinger, the system worked because it not only established a solid balance of power between the major European players, but was also based on a shared sense of legitimacy. As Kissinger eloquently puts it: "The balance of power reduces the opportunities for using force; a shared sense of justice reduces the desire to use force".[41] The Congress of Vienna created an international order on the continent that was based on common values but backed up by power-political constellations. Yet, as power-political circumstances started to change, the shared sense of legitimacy, from which the commitment to preserve the status quo derived, started to crumble. One cannot consist without the other, and it only required an ambitious statesman like Otto von Bismarck to turn the settlement on its head.

(g) Realpolitik

The status quo oriented settlement at Vienna, however, could not fully extinguish the revolutionary and nationalistic moods stirred by the wars against Napoleon. The 19th century was a period when nation states emerged and consolidated themselves on the continent. A key question was what would happen in Germany, that is, whether Germany as a nation would fall under the leadership of Austria as a successor to the Holy Roman Empire of the German Nation, and thus be multinational in character, or Prussia would unite Germany under its leadership.

In the second half of the 19th century, Prussia had become the strongest German state. Otto von Bismarck, who became Prime Minister of Prussia in 1862, concluded that it was time for Prussia to take on a leadership role on the Continent and claim its rightful place in accordance with its actual power. He repudiated the Holy Alliance with Austria, an alliance based on their common conservative values, and began to forge alliances and relationships with other states based not on shared ideology but on common national interests and power-political calculations.[42] For Bismarck, power was self-legitimising – a state that had the power to assert a leadership role on the continent also had the right to do so. This idea was encapsulated in Bismarck's famous principle of realpolitik.[43]

However, as Kissinger cautions, the pursuit of realpolitik by the major powers in an international system only prevents hostile confrontations as long as the players are free to change allies in accordance with the changing balance of power, and/or are restrained by an internationally agreed system of norms and values.[44] Neither was the case in continental Europe, with dire consequences. As Kissinger explains, "the literal application of *Realpolitik* led to the...excessive dependence on military power, and from there to an armament race and two world wars".[45] Bismarck's successors lacked the moderation that Bismarck displayed. Moreover, the Concert of Europe fell into irrelevance by the mid-19th century and no longer acted as a restraint on Great Power ambitions.[46]

(h) The Two World Wars and the Emerging Concept of Collective Security

There have been endless debates about the exact causes of World War I. By the time the war started, Europe's Great Powers had entangled themselves in either one of the Continent's two alliances. By 1914, a united Germany and Austria-Hungary found themselves head-to-head with the Triple Entente made up of Britain, France and Russia. Through a rapid series of events, all major powers were eventually drawn into the war due to collective defence agreements signed by the members of each of the two alliances.

It was the entry of the United States into the war that eventually put an end to it, and it was the US view of international politics and the US interpretation of what caused World War I that shaped the post-war settlement enshrined in the Treaty of Versailles. This section is primarily interested in the lessons that statesmen drew from World War I and how these lessons were reflected in the post-war settlement aimed at securing the peace.

At Versailles, the fundamentally different views of international relations that prevailed in Europe and the United States at the time clashed with each other. At its foundation, the view promoted by President Woodrow Wilson was based on his faith in the goodness and essential peacefulness of human nature. Because human beings, by their very nature, wanted to live in peace, people would feel neither the urge nor the necessity to go to war against each other if they were able to determine the fate of their own nation.[47] Hence Wilson's famous adage that democracies do not go to war against each other.

In the US view, therefore, the nature of the domestic political system, and not just the conduct of another country's foreign policy, matters to the national security of other states. This view stood in strong contrast to the Westphalian system of non-interference in each other's domestic affairs and subsequent theories of balance of power as a way of restraining the territorial ambitions of states. The US answer to securing a peaceful world order was based on the principle of collective security. Collective security entails that all sovereign states of the world, whether large or small, would act in concert against any act of aggression or injustice committed by one state against another. In such a system, aggression a priori constitutes a violation of the rights of another state and thus needs to be opposed. In a collective security system, resisting aggression becomes a moral imperative rather than just a geopolitical necessity.

The principle of collective security fundamentally differs from the system of alliances that existed in the 19th century European balance of power system. As Kissinger explains, "Traditional alliances were directed against specific threats and defined precise obligations for specific groups of countries linked by shared national interests or mutual security concerns".[48] In contrast, the collective security system is designed to oppose any state action that endangers international peace.[49] Violation of the principle of peaceful coexistence by one state is thus seen as an a priori threat to all other states. The problem, however is that not all states within a collective security system might interpret a threat to international peace and a threat to their own national security in the same way and may not be willing to oppose aggression everywhere in the world if they do not believe their individual national interest to be at stake.

While the European pre-war order based on alliances and the balance of power rested on the premise that the national interests of states differed from each other fundamentally and needed to be reconciled and balanced out through diplomacy and agreements, Wilson's collective security system was based on the belief that all states in essence had the same interests at heart, as the great majority of human beings living in these states were by nature peace-loving.[50]

At Versailles, President Wilson introduced his famous Fourteen Points, eight of which were classified as "obligatory" to secure the peace. These points included open diplomacy, freedom of the seas, free trade, general arms reduction, the impartial settlement of colonial claims, the return of conquered Russian territories to Russia, and the creation of a "general association of nations…formed under specific covenants for the purpose of affording mutual guarantees of political independence and territorial integrity to great and small states alike" – which was to become the League of Nations, the centrepiece of the collective security system.[51]

Ultimately, however, the Treaty of Versailles was strongly influenced by the attitudes of the United States' European allies, notably France, which sought to punish Germany extremely harshly. Article 231 of the Treaty of Versailles, the so-called "War Guilt clause", attributed sole responsibility for the war to Germany. From this article followed a series of punitive measures against Germany, including massive reparation payments and German disarmament.[52] However, the measures imposed were so harsh that they were never fully enforced. Germany was thus left psychologically humiliated but not weakened enough to prevent its re-emergence. It was a highly dangerous way of dealing with a former aggressor state. Germany's deep sense of humiliation coupled with the reluctance of the European powers to enforce the harsh terms of the Treaty of Versailles provided the opportunity for Adolf Hitler to emerge as a new German leader by promising to make Germany great again. Moreover, the League of Nations, set up to uphold the integrity of international state borders, was rendered ineffective from the start by the US Senate's refusal to ratify the Versailles treaty, which kept the US out of the League. Hence, the League was deprived of effective enforcement capabilities to counter aggression around the world.

(i) Towards a Common European Security Policy

After the end of World War II, a new collective security system was set up based on the creation of a successor organisation to the League of Nations, the United Nations (UN). The UN proved to be much more effective than the League because the world's major powers were among its members. Moreover, the UN Security Council reflected the international power structure of 1945, with the United States, the United Kingdom (UK), France, China and the Soviet Union retaining veto powers. The United Nations Security Council was also able to authorise the use of force following a perceived breach of international peace and security.

In Western Europe, balance of power gave way to cooperation and collective security. The emergence of Soviet satellite states in Eastern Europe and the onset of the Cold War led the United States and the Western European powers to create a collective defence organisation, the North Atlantic Treaty Organization (NATO), in 1949. The NATO charter stipulates that each member country will consider an attack on one member state to be an attack on all. Furthermore, the former arch-rivals, Germany and France, together with four other Western European countries formed the European Coal and Steel Community (ECSC) in 1952, which regulated the sharing of coal and steel resources among its members. The community, which secured access to these key strategic and economic resources, removed an important incentive for the conquest of territory, and close economic interaction helped to ease tensions among the former warring parties. The ECSC became the European Economic Community (EEC) in 1957 and the European Union (EU) in 1993, which in 2007 has 27 member states. EU member states not only share a common market, but are also working on a common foreign and security policy (CFSP).[53]

The European Security Strategy, published in 2003, is multi-pronged, taking into account the complexity of today's security threats. For example, it envisages the use of economic pressure and incentives to change the behaviour of proliferators of weapons of mass destruction; it calls for the employment of a "mixture of intelligence, police, judicial, military and other means" to tackle terrorism; and it advocates the use of military power and effective policing, along with humanitarian and economic assistance, to deal with state failure.[54]

The European Security Strategy places a lot of emphasis on well-functioning global institutions and international law to enhance global – and with it EU – security. It makes the strengthening of the United Nations one of its key priorities, because the UN provides the framework for the international legal system, and its Security Council is endowed with the mandate to maintain, and if necessary enforce, international peace and security.[55] It also welcomes the broadening of the membership of international financial and economic institutions, such as the World Trade Organization (WTO), as a way of promoting global prosperity.[56]

Unlike the 19th century British notion of balance of power, which did not concern itself with the internal condition and political system of other states, the European Security Strategy makes a strong connection between the domestic situation in states and international security. It maintains that the international system can only be as strong and predictable as the individual national governments that make up the system. The European Security Strategy thus states: "The best protection for our security is a world of well-governed democratic states. Spreading good governance, supporting social and political reform, dealing with corruption and abuse of power, establishing the rule of law and protecting human rights are the best means of strengthening the international order."[57]

As well as addressing global threats, the European Security Strategy is concerned with regional security issues. The EU's neighbourhood policy rests on the premise that increased peace and prosperity among countries bordering the EU will enhance EU security. Again, it makes a connection between EU security and the domestic security condition of its neighbours: "Neighbours who are engaged in violent conflict, weak states where organized crime flourishes, dysfunctional societies or exploding population growth on its borders all pose problems for Europe".[58] Hence, the EU sees the promotion of a "ring of well governed countries" along its borders and around the Mediterranean as a lynchpin of its security policy.[59] In particular, it considers the resolution of the Arab-Israeli conflict to be a key priority.

The decision of states to cooperate so closely in security matters, however, comes at a price. A country that enters a collective security organisation may benefit from increased protection and security, but gives up part of its ability to define an individual national security policy of its own. When security-related decisions are increasingly being made by an international body, national lawmakers have less of a say in this area of policy making. Clearly, the European Security Strategy is based on the notion that all member states in essence share the same security needs and priorities.

An Austrian study comparing the security strategies of EU member states suggests that Europeans share a variety of security interests in common.[60] The proliferation of weapons of mass destruction and international terrorism have had the highest priority among EU member states in recent years, and joint policies in these two areas have already been worked out in great detail. According to the study, other common European security objectives that have not yet been worked out sufficiently at the EU level are arms control, energy security, the fight against international organised crime, disease control and the fight against illegal migration. At the same time, the study notes that strategic priorities regarding the EU neighbourhood differ among members, depending on the geographic location of the individual state.[61]

Moreover, it might be easier for states to agree on long-term security objectives than on short-term policy priorities and the means to achieve them. The EU is attempting a delicate balancing act by taking into account the needs and wishes of individual member states while at the same time trying to ensure that they do not paralyse the EU's ability to take decisive policy decisions. The extent to which EU member states will be able to implement a common security policy in the coming years remains to be seen.

(j) Soviet and Russian National Security Concepts

After the Russian Revolution and the establishment of a communist regime, the overriding security imperative for the new Soviet leadership under Vladimir I. Lenin was the defence of Soviet territory and the preservation of the communist system at home.[62] His successor, Joseph Stalin, introduced the concept of the world being divided into two diametrically opposed camps – the capitalist / imperialist and the communist world – and he believed that war between the two camps was ultimately inevitable. Nikita S. Khrushchev (1953-64) modified this view, arguing that peaceful coexistence between the two camps was possible – particularly because the Soviet Union had acquired enough nuclear deterrence capabilities to ward off a US attack.[63] Khrushchev still expected socialism to ultimately prevail in the world, but believed that socialism could advance without a major war between the United States and the Soviet Union. In 1973, Leonid Breshnev proclaimed that peaceful coexistence would remain a permanent state of relations between the communist and capitalist camps.[64] By the late 1980s, Soviet military doctrine had turned into a defensive concept of "reasonable sufficiency", which meant that the Soviet military was to be strong enough to ensure national security but not to engage in offensive military operations.[65]

The dissolution of the Soviet Union made it necessary for its successor state, the Russian Federation, to formulate a new security doctrine. The country issued an interim policy document in 1993, which defined the security imperatives of the new state. The overarching theme of the policy document is the need to maintain domestic stability and secure borders so that the Russian Federation can consolidate itself. The document also acknowledges that the Russian military, unlike the Soviet forces, no longer has global imperial ambitions, but sees its role as a regional military power. The new security doctrine placed emphasis on keeping Russia's border areas peaceful and thus called for a restructuring of Russian forces so that they could be quickly deployed to end regional conflicts.[66]

In December 1997, Russian President Boris Yeltsin approved the National Security Concept of the Russian Federation. At its core, the concept states that the most significant threats to Russian security were coming from inside the country, not from the outside, and that economic decline, political instability and social problems, such as public health issues and unemployment, were threatening internal peace and stability.[67] Economic reform is thus made the pre-eminent security priority. The doctrine takes a comprehensive view of security and considers not only narrow state interests, but also the security of society and individuals.[68] This means, at the individual level, that individual rights and freedoms are protected, personal safety is guaranteed, individual living standards are enhanced and "opportunities for physical, spiritual and intellectual development abound".[69] At the societal level, the document stresses the preservation of democracy and social peace and the promotion of the nation's spiritual revival.[70] It acknowledges that without an internally cohesive, educated and prosperous society, Russia will not be able to project its power outwards and engage in an active foreign policy.[71] In the foreign policy sphere, the concept stresses the need for cooperation with foreign countries and international institutions as a way of enhancing Russia's physical security and economic prosperity.[72]

In 2000, Russian President Vladimir Putin issued a new National Security Concept, which adopts a more assertive tone. While the 1997 strategy saw Russia's relationship with the West as a partnership, the 2000 concept sees it as a rivalry between Russia's vision of a multi-polar world and the West under the leadership of the United States, which is seen as bent on dominating the world.[73] Although the document still places a lot of emphasis on internal threats to Russian security, it also includes a substantial list of external threats, such as WMD proliferation, territorial claims against Russia and NATO's eastward expansion.[74] As one expert notes, internal threats from terrorism and separatism are linked to external threats, and the concept "argues that international terrorism involves efforts to undermine the sovereignty and territorial integrity of Russia, with the possibility of direct military aggression".[75] As a result, the new concept places renewed emphasis on more traditional security instruments, that is, national military defence. It thereby stresses Russia's need to invest in scientific and technological research to keep up with the latest military technology.[76] Nonetheless, Russia's security concept continues to emphasise that national security "can only be achieved by the development of Russia's economy", which requires continued integration into the world economy.[77]

2. US National Security Doctrines

Throughout its history, the United States, today's only superpower, has put forward a series of national security doctrines that sought to adjust US national security policy to changing geopolitical circumstances. Nonetheless, there have been strong continuities throughout. There has been the lasting tension between isolationism, the notion of the United States as the City on the Hill that leads by example and concentrates on building a perfect democracy at home, and the idea of Manifest Destiny, the belief that the United States has a unique mission in the world to spread democracy and human rights beyond its borders. This section describes the United States' major security doctrines that helped to guide the foreign policy of successive US presidents.

(a) George Washington's Farewell Address

As George Washington ended his second and final term as the first President of the United States in 1796, he published an open letter to the nation known today as the Farewell Address. The address was delivered at a time when the United States consisted of a small patch of territory on the east coast of North America, while the rest of the continent was occupied by France, Great Britain and Spain or inhabited by indigenous tribes.[78] Washington at the time recognised that it was in the national security interest of the United States for the great powers of Europe to remain distracted by their own rivalries and quarrels, and the United States thus pursued a policy of neutrality. He stated that the United States should not let itself be guided by sympathies towards any power: "Permanent inveterate antipathies against particular Nations, and passionate attachments for others, should be excluded," he wrote, adding that US foreign policy should instead be driven by its interests.[79] He wanted the United States to forge economic ties with other states, but without favouring any nation over the other and without translating economic relations into political commitments. He advised that the United States could only pursue its genuine interests if it "steer[ed] clear of permanent alliances with any portion of the foreign world",[80] and thereby retained as much freedom of action as possible. "Why," he asked rhetorically, "by interweaving our destiny with that of any part of Europe, entangle our peace and prosperity in the toils of European ambition, rivalship, interest, humor or caprice?"[81] By keeping out of European politics, Washington explained, the United States, well protected by two oceans, could concentrate all its efforts and energy on building up and strengthening its still young domestic institutions,[82] as well as expanding its own presence on the North American continent.[83]

(b) The Monroe Doctrine

In 1823, US President James Monroe took the foreign policy principles outlined in Washington's Farewell Address one step further by formulating the so-called Monroe Doctrine. Monroe declared that "we should consider any attempt on the . . . part [of European powers] to extend their system to any portion of this hemisphere as dangerous to our peace and safety."[84] The doctrine emerged in the aftermath of the Napoleonic wars, following which Spain lost its colonial possessions in South America. There were fears that Spain, in alliance with France and with the backing of the Holy Alliance (Russia, Prussia and Austria), would intervene in an attempt to regain the territories of the newly independent Latin American republics. President Monroe thereby rejected British offers to intervene to prevent powers like France and Russia from gaining a foothold on the American continent. Instead, he affirmed the independence of US foreign policy, insisting that both the United States and the European powers stay out of each others' affairs.[85] Although the United States at the time lacked the necessary military strength to enforce the doctrine, the United States was fortunate that it was also in the interests of Great Britain, with its powerful navy, to keep other European powers out of the Western hemisphere.[86]

(c) Westward Expansion and the Concept of Manifest Destiny

The notion of Manifest Destiny was formulated by the influential US columnist John L. O'Sullivan in 1839 "to explain and justify the westward expansion of the United States".[87] Sullivan stated that it was the United States' divine destiny to spread its founding principles of equality and human liberty, which were universal values that all human beings deserved to enjoy. He wrote:

> We are the nation of human progress, and who will, what can, set limits to our onward march? Providence is with us, and no earthly power can. We point to the everlasting truth on the first page of our national declaration, and we proclaim to the millions of other lands that 'the gates of hell' – the powers of aristocracy and monarchy – shall not prevail against it.[88]

At the same time, US expansion on the North American continent served an important national security objective. By controlling the entire mid-section of the North American continent from the Atlantic coast to the Pacific coast, the United States occupied an ideal geopolitical position. The two oceans not only protected the borders of the United States, they also provided new opportunities for trade and the expansion of US influence abroad.

The three doctrines described above complemented each other and defined US national security policy until the early 20th century. They allowed the United States to strengthen its domestic institutions, and to expand and consolidate its geopolitical position while staying out of entanglements abroad. Once the United States became a strong geopolitical presence, however, its national security policy needed to be modified to adjust to the new circumstances.

(d) "Open Door": Building US Naval Power

In 1890, the US naval historian and strategist Alfred Thayer Mahan published the highly influential book *The Influence of Sea Power Upon History.* In the book, Mahan argues that all great powers throughout history had maintained a strong navy and strong merchant marines.[89] He thereby urged the United States to build its own navy and claim its rightful place in the world.[90] At the time the book was published, the United States was already becoming a Pacific and Asian power, taking over Hawaii, Guam, Wake Island and, in 1898, the Philippines. The Spanish-American War of 1898, which resulted in US victories in both Cuba and the Far East, helped to strengthen the geopolitical position of the United States.[91] Mahan argued that the United States could not protect its acquisitions and commercial interests abroad by maintaining its defensive, Western hemisphere-centric posture. Mahan warned that if the United States did not control its oceans, enemy powers would do so, threatening both US national security and its overseas possessions.[92]

The United States partly endorsed Mahan's theory with the promulgation of the "Open Door Policy" in 1898. The term was initially created by the British during the division of Chinese trading rights, and stipulated that each nation should have the same commercial rights in China as every other nation. In practice, as political scientist Francis Sempa explains, the policy was "a doctrine of overseas commercial and political expansion. To be effective, the Open Door required strong US naval power".[93] Theodore Roosevelt, who became

US President in 1901, shared Mahan's belief in the importance of a strong navy and strongly endorsed the Open Door Policy. He greatly expanded US naval power and pursued an activist Open Door policy in Asia.[94] He also initiated the construction of the Panama Canal and strengthened US dominance in the Caribbean.[95]

(e) The Two World Wars and the US Role as an Offshore Balancer

The decision by President Woodrow Wilson in 1917 to enter World War I on the side of Britain, France and Russia marked the beginning of a new national security doctrine in the United States – a doctrine that was to define US foreign policy until 1945. Sempa aptly describes the new role the United States was embracing as that of an Offshore Balancer.[96] The new doctrine relied on the premise that the overpowering dominance of one power over large areas in either Europe or Asia would eventually pose a threat to US national security. During World War I, the United States decided to intervene out of fear of German continental hegemony. However, it did so rather reluctantly. Intervention was considered a measure of last resort, and the United States left the continent as soon as the war was over and a peace settlement had been reached.[97] The isolationist impulses cultivated during the 19th century remained a strong undercurrent in US foreign policy thinking, and isolationism ultimately prevailed in the US Senate when Wilson failed to get the necessary majority to keep the United States involved in the collective security arrangement set up at Versailles.

The United States also reluctantly assumed the role of an offshore balancer during World War II. President Franklin D. Roosevelt had recognised the threat posed by Nazi Germany early and provided as much assistance to Britain, short of direct military aid, as he could without having to secure approval from the US Senate, in which the majority was opposed to direct US intervention on the continent. In fact, it required a direct attack by Japan on the US military base at Pearl Harbor and the subsequent declaration of war by Japan's ally Germany on the United States for Roosevelt to obtain the necessary approval to enter the war against the Axis powers.

(f) The Beginning of the Cold War and the Policy of Containment

After the end of World War II, the United States expected to withdraw its troops from the continent within a few years and to allow the newly created United Nations to watch over the peace. However, a series of threatening moves by the Soviet Union convinced the United States that it needed to assume a more activist role. By early 1946, the US administration under President Harry Truman became alerted to Soviet expansionist ambitions by massive Soviet troop movements into northern Iran, Stalin's request for a role in the occupation of Japan, and the creation of Soviet puppet regimes in Eastern Europe. Moreover, in early February 1946, Stalin made a threatening speech asserting that war between the communist and the capitalist camps would be inevitable in the long term.

In the wake of these hostile Soviet gestures, George F. Kennan, a specialist in Russian affairs and chargé d'affaires in the US embassy in Moscow, sent a telegram to Washington with a well-informed analysis of Soviet behaviour and motives, which became known as Kennan's "Long Telegram". In the telegram, dated 22 February 1946, Kennan warned that behind the guise of Soviet communist ideology lay hidden a century-old Russian sense of insecurity coupled with traditional tsarist expansionist ambitions. Unable to tolerate the existence of independent centres of power along its frontiers, Moscow was relentlessly seeking to export communism abroad and to subsequently dominate newly emerging communist countries. According to Kennan, the United States had no other choice but to politically ostracise the Soviet Union, to foster national cohesion at home, and to provide ideological and political guidance to other non-communist countries to prevent them from falling into the Soviet orbit.

Kennan suggested that "the main element of any United States policy toward the Soviet Union must be that of long-term, patient but firm and vigilant containment of Russian expansive tendencies".[98] Kennan's analysis gave Truman's already hardening policy towards the Soviet Union an intellectual justification and gave rise to a new US national security doctrine based on the principle of containment.

Truman made the shift in US foreign policy explicit in a speech before the US Congress in 1947, when he asked Congress to approve US economic and military aid for Greece and Turkey to prevent the countries from falling into the Soviet orbit – which he implied would ultimately jeopardise US security. In what is today known as the Truman Doctrine, Truman asserted that the United States needed to actively oppose the spread of communism: "I believe that it must be the policy of the United States to support free peoples who are resisting attempted subjugation by armed minorities or by outside pressures". He added:

> The free peoples of the world look to us for support in maintaining their freedoms. If we falter in our leadership, we may endanger the peace of the world – and we shall surely endanger the welfare of our own nation. Great responsibilities have been placed upon us by the swift movement of events.[99]

The Marshall plan and the creation of NATO followed in 1949, which were means of economic and military containment, respectively. Through the formation of NATO, the United States committed itself to the defence of Western Europe and stationed US troops on the continent. The successful detonation of a Soviet Atomic device in August 1949 alarmed the United States, which until that time had a nuclear monopoly. The event led Truman to ask Paul Nitze, head of the State Department's Policy Planning Staff, to reassess US foreign policy, taking into account the impact of the Soviet possession of an atomic bomb on US national security and the role of the United States as a world power. The document that emerged from Nitze's extensive study in April 1950, commonly known as NSC-68, became the first comprehensive US foreign policy statement since the end of World War II.[100] The main premise of the policy statement was that maintaining US military superiority was the key to ultimate victory over the Soviet Union. Hence, the United States needed to rapidly expand its conventional and its nuclear weapons arsenals. NSC-68 thereby conveys a very one-dimensional view of "power" by focusing almost exclusively on military capabilities. This stands in contrast to Kennan's notion of containment, which included an important ideological component. He argued that US victory could be partly achieved through the promotion and strengthening of US democratic values at home and among its allies abroad. For Kennan, the Cold War could ultimately only be won politically and psychologically.

NSC-68 in essence advocated a policy that went beyond mere containment. It recommended that the United States actively promote the destruction of the Soviet Union by playing on nationalist sentiments within the Soviet Union and supporting subversive activities in Eastern Europe. In practice, however, the United States did not pursue a "roll back" policy and tacitly accepted the Soviet sphere of domination and influence. The possession of large nuclear arsenals on both sides of the Cold War prevented either from overly adventurous policies in the other's sphere of influence, and from risking a direct military confrontation.[101]

(i) Mutually Assured Destruction

In the 1950s, when the United States still had nuclear superiority, President Eisenhower endorsed a strategy of "massive retaliation", stating that the United States would make full use of its nuclear weapons in case of a Soviet conventional or nuclear attack on Western Europe. By the 1960s, however, the Soviet Union had developed its nuclear capabilities enough for the United States to be no longer in a position to destroy the entire Soviet nuclear arsenal in a first strike. It would thus have risked a second, retaliatory, strike by the Soviet Union on US territory. As a consequence, the concept of nuclear deterrence gave rise to the military strategy of Mutually Assured Destruction (MAD). The strategy is based on the notion that a nuclear exchange between the United States and the Soviet Union would lead to the destruction of both countries – regardless of which power launched the first strike – and it was thus in neither power's interest to attack the other country. MAD implied the accumulation of nuclear stockpiles by both sides in the Cold War so that the costs would be too high for either side to ever make use of them.[102]

(ii) Realism in the post-World War II Era

Realist political thought, in and of itself a European "invention", established itself as an intellectual current in US foreign policy thinking in the post-World War II era. Political theorist Hans Morgenthau, who left Nazi Germany as a young man and emigrated to the United States in the 1930s, became one of the defining proponents of political realism in the United States. In his work, he solidified the connection between national security and realism by defining national interest in terms of power. For Morgenthau, the national interest of states equalled national security based on the projection of power,[103] and he advised that "The statesman must think in terms of the national interest, conceived as power among other powers".[104] Echoing Morgenthau, Kennan argued that it was dangerous for states to wage wars for other than strategic objectives. In his 1950 book *American Diplomacy*, Kennan criticised the US "moralistic-legalistic" approach to foreign policy for setting the bar too high by forcing a country to go beyond just pursuing its national security objectives and instead seek "total domination" of its enemy. He called on US leaders to "admit that our own national interest is all we are really capable of knowing and understanding".[105] Realist thinkers in the United States thus rejected the idealist notion that the United States had a divine mandate to liberate peoples and spread democracy. Instead, realists like Kennan maintained that the world would be a much safer place if countries would not try to achieve moral objectives through their foreign policy but instead focused on their more measurable national security needs.

(iii) Détente

Realism strongly defined US foreign policy in the early 1970s, when President Richard Nixon and his Secretary of State and National Security Adviser Henry Kissinger took a new approach to the policy of containment. Nixon refused to see the struggle between the Soviet Union and the United States in black and white terms. He de-emphasised the ideological component of the confrontation and instead dealt with the Soviet Union as a geopolitical menace, and as a country pursuing its national interest like any other power.[106] By dropping its moralistic approach towards the Soviet Union, the Nixon administration gained much more negotiating flexibility. As a result of a series of dialogues with the Soviet Union, the United States was able to greatly reduce tensions between the East and the West.

The policy is popularly known as the policy of détente or "peaceful coexistence". Détente was partly a consequence of Kissinger's Realist approach to foreign policy but, more importantly, it grew out of the realisation that the United States was unable to sustain and continue the arms race with the Soviet Union and keep up large military engagements such as the costly war in Vietnam, which was fought in the name of containment. The United States needed some form of accommodation with the Soviet Union. Similarly, the Soviet Union was feeling the heavy financial burden of the nuclear arms race and worried about the decline in its geopolitical position as a result of the Sino-Soviet split and Nixon's subsequent rapprochement with China. Having achieved rough nuclear parity, the two countries knew that there was no longer a military option for ending the Cold War. The result of the policy of détente was a series of arms control agreements, a relaxation of tensions in Europe, and the expansion of trade between the United States and the Soviet Union.

(g) Going Beyond Containment: Liberation and Roll-back

Under the Presidency of Ronald Reagan, the relatively passive Cold War policy of containment changed to a more activist policy of "liberation". Reagan's National Security Decision Directive 75 (NSDD-75) of 1982 states that the United States should "contain and over time reverse Soviet expansionism" and try to "loosen Moscow's hold" on Eastern Europe.[107] This came partly in response to a series of offensive Soviet moves. In late 1977, the Soviet Union started to deploy SS-20 missiles and mobile launchers in its western republics. The SS-20 was a modern intermediate-range missile with the capability of launching three independently targeted nuclear weapons. The missiles posed a clear threat to Western Europe and thus changed the balance of power on the continent.[108] In 1979, the Soviet Union invaded Afghanistan. The Soviets did so to prop up the communist government in Afghanistan, which was set up in the 1970s but was on the verge of collapse due to a lack of popular support. Taking control of the country was also a way for the Soviet Union to expand its influence and protect its interests in Asia.[109] The Soviet army, however, encountered fierce resistance from the Afghan people and, after taking control of the capital Kabul, became bogged down in efforts to control the Afghan countryside.

In the light of these Soviet moves, many in the United States started to feel that the United States was losing out in the Cold War and that mere containment was no longer enough to counter an increasingly emboldened Soviet Union. The newly elected President Reagan agreed with this view. In his 1985 State of the Union Address, Reagan formulated what was later called the "Reagan Doctrine", which stated that the United States would support anti-communist insurgencies anywhere in the world.[110] The new national security doctrine led the United States to support anti-communist fighters in Afghanistan, Nicaragua and other Third World countries, and to support dissidents in Eastern Europe.[111] Reagan's massive military build-up and the Strategic Defense Initiative (SDI) were ways of enhancing US military superiority vis-à-vis the Soviet Union. The goal of the United States shifted from mere containment to an attempt to "bring down the Soviet Empire".[112] Although some have criticised Reagan's moralistic and militant Cold War approach as highly dangerous, others have argued that Reagan's renewed arms race forced the Soviet Union, unable to match US military spending without facing bankruptcy, to eventually abandon its empire.

(h) The 1990s Interlude

The collapse of the Soviet Union fundamentally changed the global security environment, and the United States no longer saw itself head-to-head with a hostile superpower. On the contrary, the United States was now the world's only superpower and its military might was unparalleled. In the 1990s, President Bill Clinton presided over a period or relative peace, and his administration advocated the idea that as the world's most powerful nation, the United States had a responsibility to protect human lives in countries and places where governments were either unable or unwilling to do so. As a result, the United States became increasingly involved in humanitarian interventions and nation building, with mixed results. Examples were the US intervention in Somalia and NATO interventions in Bosnia and Kosovo. The brutal conflict in the former Yugoslav republic of Bosnia-Herzegovina, for example, led President Clinton to send 20,000 US troops as part of a 60,000-strong NATO contingent to Bosnia to enforce the peace and provide a safe environment for elections to take place.[113] The challenge that the United States was facing was that the humanitarian crises in most cases took place within states. Yet, the Clinton administration maintained that the moral imperative to save lives trumped the obligation under international law to respect the sovereignty of these states. Besides increased involvement in humanitarian interventions in the 1990s, however, no encompassing national security doctrine defined US strategy in the post-Cold War world.

(i) The "War on Terrorism" and the Policy of Pre-emption

The relatively quiet foreign policy interlude of the 1990s was brought to an abrupt halt with the terrorist attacks on the United States of 11 September 2001, which powerfully demonstrated the threat that a small but well-organised group of people could pose to the country. Meanwhile, US intelligence estimates were concluding that hostile countries such as North Korea, Iraq and Iran were seeking to acquire WMD, which further convinced the United States that a new set of dangers was threatening national security.[114] The new enemies were now rogue states and non-state actors with an intensely hostile anti-US posture and the determination to acquire and possibly use WMD.

From these events came the realisation that the United States had to be proactive to prevent hostile entities from acquiring WMD before they could pose a threat to US territory. In his National Security Strategy (NSS) published in September 2002, President George

W. Bush announced a new security doctrine based on pre-empting attacks from hostile nations. The first manifestation of Bush's new policy of pre-emption was the war in Iraq in 2003, based partly on the argument that Saddam Hussein's regime was developing WMD and needed to be stopped before it was too late. As Sempa explains, "Bush did not claim that Iraq's threat to use or transfer such weapons to terrorists was 'imminent'. In fact the rationale behind the Pre-emption doctrine is that the United States can no longer afford to wait until such threats are imminent."[115]

According to the 2002 National Security Strategy, the enemies that the United States was confronted with differ fundamentally from the Soviet menace during the Cold War. While the Soviet Union considered the use of WMD to be a measure of last resort and was in many ways "risk-averse", rogue nations and terrorist groups have few scruples about using them. The NSS concludes that "Traditional concepts of deterrence will not work against a terrorist enemy whose avowed tactics are wanton destruction and the targeting of innocents".[116]

Part of the new policy of pre-emption is the notion that the United States cannot afford to feel constrained when it comes to its national security and is willing to act alone. Some scholars have pointed out that a broad application of the pre-emption doctrine is dangerous because it might lead the United States to opt for military action too fast and before other avenues for resolving conflicts have been thoroughly explored.[117]

(j) Defending Peace and Prosperity

In congruence with long-held US foreign policy tradition, President George W. Bush stressed in a speech in 2002 that "Our nation's cause has always been larger than our nation's defense".[118] Bush thus reiterated a conviction, shared by the Founding Fathers, that the United States had a special mission in the world that went beyond just protecting its own state borders. An important aspect of the 2002 US NSS is thus to support the spread of political and economic freedom and human dignity around the world. The NSS stresses the universality of these values: "the United States must defend liberty and justice because these principles are right and true for all people everywhere. No nation owns these aspirations, and no nation is exempt from them".[119] The NSS recognises that terrorists and tyrants partly are bred in conditions of political oppression and economic scarcity. Giving more people political freedoms and economic opportunities would help to eliminate an important source of these types of threats to the United States. The US NSS also makes a connection between extreme poverty and state failure, and with it an unstable international order. It therefore implies that the United States could ultimately only be safe if the rest of the world enjoyed an adequate level of economic prosperity and political freedom. At the same time, however, the NSS suggests that the United States will promote democracy and human rights first and foremost because it is the "right thing to do"; and as the United States now has the means and power to change the world for the better, it has a special obligation to work for these universal human values.

George W. Bush updated the US NSS at the start of his second term of office and made the promotion of freedom and democracy a cornerstone of his second administration's security agenda. Bush's 2006 NSS argues that "the fundamental character of regimes matters as much as the distribution of power among them".[120] It states that the goal of US foreign policy is to spread democracy and principles of good governance around the world, because it is "the best way to provide enduring security for the American people".[121] The 2006 NSS therefore strongly follows the Manifest Destiny tradition in US foreign policy thinking, based on the notion that the United States has a special mission to extinguish tyranny around the world. Only if all people in the world can live in freedom, the new NSS implies, can the United States be truly secure.

3. Security Doctrines in Japan and China

Having examined above the security strategies that the United States and some of the major European countries have pursued over the past few centuries, this section briefly outlines the approaches to national security of two major powers in Asia – Japan and China.

(a) Japan's Multidimensional Approach to Security

The defining characteristic of Japanese security thinking since the emergence of the modern Japanese state in the second part of the 19th century has been an emphasis on the interrelationship between economic prosperity and security.[122] In the mind of the Japanese, economics cannot be divorced from social contexts – a notion derived from Confucianism.

(i) Economic Prosperity and National Security

The term *keizai* (the literal translation of which is "administrating the nation and relieving the suffering of the people") was coined during the Tokugawa Shogunate (1603-1867).[123] The Japanese elite retained the notion that a well-managed national economy and state stability went hand-in-hand also during the Meiji period (1868-1912). During this period, Japan embarked on an ambitious industrialisation programme along with building a strong and unified nation state. The Meijis believed that building a wealthy nation and a strong army was the only way for Japan to avoid colonisation by imperial Western powers.[124] Following the Meiji period, the ruling elites in the Taisho and Showa periods equally stressed the importance of an economically and militarily strong Japan to ensuring the survival and independence of the state. However, they maintained that the long-term survival of the state could only be guaranteed if Japan had reliable access to the natural resources required for Japan's industrialisation, as well as access to foreign markets. The Japanese elite in the 1920-1940s thus sought to create a so-called Greater East Asia Co-Prosperity Sphere and began its process of regional imperial expansion, which eventually ended in the defeat of the Japanese's army and subsequent occupation of Japan by the United States in 1945.

(ii) Anti-militarism after World War II

Following Japan's crushing defeat in World War II, which ended with nuclear bombs being dropped on Hiroshima and Nagasaki, many Japanese developed a strong aversion to the military, which had brought so much suffering to the nation. Furthermore, the Japanese continued to hold on to their traditional belief that a strong military alone was not sufficient to maintaining national security.

Article 9 of the Japanese Constitution, drawn up by the US post-war occupation authorities, explicitly outlaws war as a means of Japan's national security policy. Moreover, the constitution limits Japanese defence expenditure to one percent of gross national product (GNP) and outlaws the acquisition of nuclear weapon capabilities.[125]

Without rebuilding its national army, the Japanese nonetheless enjoyed reliable military protection after World War II. The country benefited from the military umbrella of its occupying power, the United States, which considered a strong and prosperous Japan to be an important pillar in the emerging Cold War with regard to its efforts to keep Soviet and Chinese communist influence at bay in East Asia. Especially with the beginning of the Korean War in 1950, the United States recognised the strategic importance of a prosperous and strong Japan as an important source of supplies for the US army fighting in Korea. In 1951, Japan and the United States signed a security treaty, which allowed Japan to maintain a small self-defence force (SDF) and provided US security guarantees at a time when Cold War pressures in East Asia were mounting.[126] The treaty specifies that Japan's SDF is strictly to be used to defend Japan's territorial integrity, excluding participation in collective defence operations abroad. The SDF was placed under strict civilian supervision.[127]

The US military security guarantees, the pervasive anti-militarism in Japan after the war, and the traditional Japanese notion of the interrelationship between economics and security served as the context for the emergence of the so-called "Yoshida Doctrine". The doctrine, named after Japan's post-war Prime Minister Shigeru Yoshida, stated that while military power was necessary to defend the country, Japan would primarily pursue national security through economic means.[128] Yoshida and many others in Japan at the time believed that the emergence of Japanese militarism in the 1930s and the subsequent pursuit of overseas military expansion had been caused by the domestic economic instability that plagued the country in the 1930s. Economic instability, Japanese post-war policy makers believed, translated into social and political instability and ultimately violent conflict.[129]

During the Cold War, Japan pursued an essentially isolationist security strategy that rested on two pillars: pursuing good economic relationships in East Asia and beyond while refraining from political commitments in international security affairs; and placing Japan's regional security in the hands of its security guarantor – the United States.[130] At the same time, Japan concentrated on developing its domestic economy and state infrastructure as a way of promoting social peace and political stability.[131]

Japan has since applied the same principle of the interrelationship between economics and social peace to countries beyond Japan. After World War II, several nations in East Asia achieved independence from Western colonialism. These states were very weak and plagued by internal ethnic conflicts and political turmoil. Japan believed that only by helping to strengthen these countries' economies could their stability, and thus the stability of the region, be guaranteed.[132] Certainly, Japan's policy of creating strong economic ties with these newly sovereign states benefited Japan's own economy and re-established Japan's pre-eminence in East Asia. However, the policy also reflected subsequent Japanese leaders' genuine belief that economic development would strengthen and stabilise these states.[133] Japan intensified its aid to North-east and Southeast Asian countries in the 1970s (many of them US Cold War allies) by investing in the development of these countries' industrial infrastructures to promote long-term economic growth and domestic political stability.

Interestingly, Japan even extended economic support to its former enemy and regional military superpower, China, as a way of helping to enhance the country's internal political stability. As Hughes eloquently puts it: "There was only one threat greater to Japan than a strong China, and that was a weak one, with all its attendant problems of civil strife and unpredictable external relations".[134]

(iii) The Adoption of a Stronger Defence Posture after the Cold War

The end of the Cold War heightened concerns in Japan that the US commitment to serve as a guarantor of Japan's military security might no longer be as strong as before, and Japan feared a partial withdrawal of US military forces from East Asia. Japan's sense of insecurity was heightened by the rapid rise of China as an ever stronger economic and military power, as well as the hostile posture of North Korea. These developments led Japan to reassess its pacifistic international security strategy.[135]

An important event at the start of Japan's security policy reassessment process was the 1991 Gulf War. The war demonstrated clearly that military power continued to shape international relations in the post-Cold War environment.[136] The experience also taught Japan about the need to adopt a more global view of security and that the country was ill-equipped to deal with the type of post-Cold War crisis that the Gulf War epitomised. In fact, Japan at the time was widely criticised for its reluctance to send non-combatant personnel to the Persian Gulf.[137] Japanese policy makers thus started to look for ways to take on a more active role in international security politics.

In 1992, Japan adopted the International Peace Cooperation Law, which facilitates Japan's participation in United Nations peacekeeping operations. Japan also worked on a redefinition of the US-Japanese alliance to allow for a more active Japanese role in defence cooperation issues. The result was the new United States-Japan Joint

Security Declaration of 1996, which gave Japan a greater role in defence-related issues including missile defence and diplomacy towards China.[138] Most recently, Japan has sent unarmed SDF forces to Afghanistan and Iraq to contribute to the peacebuilding efforts in the two countries.

Japan also revised its Defence Guidelines with the United States, allowing Japanese defence forces to take part in military operations both in and outside Japan.[139] Moreover, both houses of the Japanese Parliament set up research panels to review the Peace Constitution, especially Article 9 which limits Japan to maintaining only a small self-defence force.[140] Japan's gradual strengthening of its defence capabilities in the past decade has led one observer to suggest that the country increasingly is becoming "more of a normal state – more active in both regional and international security affairs commensurate with its economic influence".[141]

At the same time, however, Japan has remained committed to its traditional, comprehensive view of security that emphasises the combination of economic and military power, while making economic power the most important security policy instrument. Indeed, Japan intensified its economic approach to security policy in the 1990s and stepped up official development assistance (ODA) to states in East Asia throughout the 1990s.[142] The East Asian financial crisis of 1997-1998 once again demonstrated to Japan how economic distress can lead to social unrest and political crises, most clearly in Indonesia.[143] In sum, Japan continues to stand out as a country that prioritises political economy approaches to security over military ones – in contrast to most other developed states today.

(b) Defending the "Middle Kingdom": China's Approach to National Security

China's consolidation as a unified state dates back to the 3rd century BC. The country has been dealing with similar types of security problems from its inception to the present day.[144] The first challenge China faces is the defence of its extremely long and vulnerable land borders. Up until the mid-19th century, China suffered from regular incursions by nomadic tribes on its periphery. After 1850, imperialist powers, including Russia, Germany, Great Britain, and France, threatened China's territorial integrity along its border area.[145] Since World War II, China has feared territorial encroachments on its periphery by major powers such as India, Russia, Japan and the United States.[146] The defence of its periphery from outside intruders has remained a key objective of Chinese security policy.

Second, the unity and stability of the Chinese state have been challenged from within throughout history. In China's political history, authority has traditionally been vested in one powerful individual, whose views and beliefs became the law of the land. As a result, China has been regularly plagued by power struggles among members of the governing elites, which often translated into domestic social upheavals. Preserving social order thus constitutes a second key objective for Chinese national security.[147]

Third, China has always seen itself as a great power. Throughout its history, the state has played a dominant role in Asia. Economically self-sufficient for centuries, China has seen itself as the "Middle Kingdom" that was culturally, socially and politically superior to its neighbours. Although, today, China seems to be pursuing equality with rather than superiority over other major powers, the preservation of its status as a great power has remained a key policy objective of the Chinese leadership.[148]

China has withdrawn from the outside world during long stretches of its history, emphasising its own cultural superiority over other peoples and nations.[149] Successive imperial regimes have tended to be highly prone to use military force to pursue strategic objectives at the height of their strength – which was usually the early part of the regimes' existence. The less stable these regimes became over time, the less willing they were to use military force, employing instead non-coercive means, including diplomatic manoeuvres, to advance their security objectives.[150] China has rarely engaged in offensive military operations. In cases where China has crossed its borders, this was to neutralise outside threats to the country's national unity and stability.[151] China would thereby always rationalise its military actions as purely defensive in nature.[152]

When the Chinese Communist Party (CCP) consolidated the country under its rule in 1949, national unity and internal stability were again the primary national security concerns of the new ruling elite. Like ancient Chinese leaders, the CCP leadership subscribed to the conviction that a strong central government was a prerequisite for maintaining internal stability.[153] Military engagements by the Chinese Army in Korea, Vietnam and elsewhere in the course of the Cold War were justified as being defensive in nature to preserve the revolution (and thus internal stability) and prevent the establishment of hostile proxy states along China's periphery. However, outside analysts may not necessarily agree that Chinese military actions were all defensive during the Cold War.

Until today, the CCP's foremost concerns have remained the unity of the nation and economic development. China's strong focus on domestic issues has often led the country to assume a passive posture in foreign affairs. For the CCP, success in building a strong and prosperous state at home has become a question of political survival. In its pursuit of "regime security" at home, the CCP does not want to be distracted by foreign embroilments.[154] On the defence front, the CCP is seeking to modernise China's armed forces to ensure the country's continued safety from outside military threats and to maintain national unity. In order to pursue its goal of building a strong and prosperous state uninterrupted, China has a vested interest in a peaceful international environment.[155] Its economic development relies on good trading relationships with other countries to attract foreign investment, acquire technological know-how and export its goods.[156]

The end of the Cold War made China's security environment more favourable. According to China expert Alastair Iain Johnston, the Chinese leadership would for the most part agree that today's security environment is "on balance, the least threatening since the founding of the People's Republic".[157] Yet, despite the more friendly security environment, China's military expenditure and efforts to modernise its armed forces have continued to increase throughout the post-Cold War era. This has presented analysts with a conundrum: "China is not balancing against any identifiable military threat at the present, and decision makers and strategists are divided about which state may constitute the next security challenge".[158] Not even the United States, which China considers to be its main rival, is regarded as an imminent military threat by Beijing. China's military build-up in the 1990s may have been an attempt to catch up with other major powers, including Russia, the United States and European powers, which all cut their military expenditure after the demise of the Soviet Union. Increased military capabilities may also serve as insurance to prepare for potential future strategic challenges.[159]

However, China's seemingly contradictory behaviour in increasing its military power at a time when the international environment appears less hostile has led one analyst to speculate that the motivation behind China's efforts to increase its military power may be less about security than status.[160] China's acquisition of nuclear weapons and its insistence on control of the South China Sea possibly reflect China's pursuit of equal status with the world's major powers. It may be an attempt to make up for the years of humiliation by the Western imperial powers that imposed "unequal treaties" on China, the memory of which is still very much alive in China.[161] As one expert explains, "Chinese foreign policy discourse since 1949 has been replete with status-related language, and foreign policy behaviour since 1949 has been aimed, in part, at protecting 'national self-respect' . . . , at enhancing China's 'international position.'"[162]

The argument that China's security policy has for the most part been defensive in nature is still quite common among experts on China, and the above summary has given several reasons to support this view. However, there are some serious counterarguments on this issue, as China has voiced its intention to expand its power and influence beyond its borders and has started to build a powerful navy. Moreover, as Johnston explains, "some Chinese strategists now also speak of the need for 'survival space' . . . and for strategic frontiers that extend horizontally into the Indian Ocean, the South China Sea, the East China Sea, and vertically into space."[163] These plans have not been created in reaction to US hegemony or to the new power-political opportunities created by the collapse of the Soviet Union. Rather, these ideas have been around at least since 1987,[164] which suggests that China is not simply reacting but has its own independent strategic agenda.

A main issue for the Chinese Government today is Taiwan. China has long claimed Taiwan as part of China, based on its interpretation of history, but there are many disagreements on this issue. At the end of the Chinese Civil War in 1949, when the communists gained control of the Chinese mainland, Taiwan served as a refuge for Chiang Kai-shek and his followers, who built up their own alternative system of government on the island in defiance of the CCP. Protected by the United States, Taiwan has been able to stay out of the Chinese communist orbit. The reunification of Taiwan with China has been a goal of the Chinese leadership ever since. China is also trying to work towards eventual reunification with Taiwan by stepping up peaceful cross-strait relations. The country continues to pursue a policy of "peaceful reunification" with Taiwan, which China considers to be part of its territory but with a different political system.

In 2004, China issued its latest comprehensive Defence White Paper, which reveals a modest shift in China's security policy posture.[165] China is obviously seeking to adapt its national strategy to the new international circumstances of a globalised world.[166] The White Paper embraces policy principles in favour of a more active foreign policy, such as engagement and international cooperation. China has also intensified its involvement in the United Nations system in recent years, and Chinese troops have participated in several UN peace-keeping operations.[167] Nevertheless, China is expected to proceed cautiously in asserting its increasing strength as a major global power. China is in no hurry: its short- and medium-term objectives are to build up national power through a strong economy and a technologically advanced military. Maintaining friendly relations with its neighbours and the major powers allows the country to pursue these goals at home and find acceptance of its geopolitical ascendance in the international community. Once the country has become stronger, analysts expect China to be more assertive in its foreign policy and military postures.[168] China's recent moves to secure access to raw materials in Africa seem to confirm this projected trend.

4. Broadening National Security Concepts

This chapter has examined the security strategies and doctrines pursued by some of the major international players. In making national security policy, every government faces the question of how to reconcile domestic national objectives and foreign security objectives. Some countries, such as China, Japan (until the late 19th century) and the United States (until World War II), have gone through long periods of isolation and maintained an inward-looking posture by focusing mainly on state consolidation and national economic development. However, all three states were eventually forced to engage with the outside world, even if just for the sake of preserving the status quo for their nation state. In today's globalised world, isolationism is no longer a viable option if a state wants to ensure long-term economic prosperity and national security. In a world where national strength at least partly depends on a country's ability to maintain strong trade relationships with other powers, and where many threats to national security can no longer be solved without cooperating with other nations, many of the national security doctrines discussed above, especially those that are based on principles of self-reliance and military self-help, can no longer be realistically pursued today. Japan's comprehensive view of security might be the most "modern" historical security doctrine discussed above. With its long experience in state building and helping other states to develop their economy as part of promoting regional stability, Japan may serve as a model for the United States and the EU, which increasingly are recognising the importance of state stability and economic security to creating a more peaceful international environment.

As is reflected in both the European Security Strategy and the latest US National Security Strategy, universal humanitarian values and the need to improve the human condition everywhere in the world are increasingly becoming central elements of foreign policy strategic thinking. This shift may partly come from the realisation that the cooperation and support of other nations that share the same values facilitate the achievement of foreign policy objectives.

Moreover, the fact that every foreign policy move of the major powers is closely scrutinised and analysed by the global media has raised the stakes for states acting in violation of international norms and laws. Having world public opinion on one's side greatly facilitates and contributes to the success of a particular foreign policy action. In other words, a state today can more easily win the sympathy and support of other states if its previous actions abroad have, for example, demonstrated a genuine concern to fight disease and poverty in the developing world.

Yet the inclusion of humanitarian causes in the foreign policy strategies of some of the world's strongest powers has not occurred simply as a new way of covering up the pursuit of traditional power-political objectives. These strategies reflect the realisation that poverty and oppression around the world can lead to violence, terrorism and many other transnational threats. Globalisation and global interdependence no longer allow us to ignore these connections. The foreign policy strategies of the world's wealthiest states today convey a sense of responsibility and moral obligation to help those less fortunate. The new foreign policy strategies also reflect a genuine concern for the well-being of humanity around the world based on our common humanity.

Having discussed different security concepts and doctrines in this chapter, chapter 3 examines the different ways in which states organise their security policy-making processes in their governments at a more practical level.

CHAPTER 3

COMPARISON OF NATIONAL SECURITY STRUCTURES AROUND THE WORLD

The security doctrines and concepts discussed in chapter 2 have served, and continue to serve, as general guidelines for statesmen when drafting security strategies and making security-related decisions, but general ideas alone do not make policy. Instead, the way the security policy-making process is organised in a specific country has an equally important influence on the policy result. Hence, this chapter is concerned with the way states organise their security policy-making process at the more practical level.

In most countries, national security consists of five major components: diplomatic, military, internal security, economic and intelligence.[169] All these components are interdependent, and a weakness in one component will adversely affect the others. In addition, there are several sub-components to national security that need to be taken into account, including "risk management, disruption control management, disaster mitigation and management . . . and consequence and national resilience management".[170] As one author puts it, "national security management is the art and technique of integrating these components and making them function in a coordinated, effective and harmonious manner in times of normalcy as well as in times of crises".[171]

How best to coordinate these diverse national security components to facilitate cooperation between different government departments is a key organisational question for any government today. Some states have created a National Security Council (NSC) to streamline the process of managing national security affairs. Although NSCs are composed differently in different states, they share common characteristics. NSCs form part of a country's executive branch and are not subject to parliamentary oversight. They serve advisory and coordinating functions rather than a policy-making function. NSCs are usually chaired by the country's president or prime minister, or headed by a person appointed by them. In the United States, this is usually the National Security Adviser, appointed by the president. The members who make up the core of the NSC usually are the heads of a country's relevant government departments and government agencies. NSCs serve the function of bringing different government officials, and sometimes heads of the armed forces and outside experts, together in one room to discuss national security issues. The meetings are, in most cases, convened at the discretion of the council chair.

NSCs help the executive branch of a government to coordinate security-related policies among the different sectors of government. For example, a coherent national security strategy can ensure that a country's economic policy towards a hostile state does not interfere with or neutralise a country's actions on the diplomatic front but instead advances the same security-related interests. Policy recommendations given by an NSC are thus likely to be free of the bureaucratic biases of one particular government department and instead represent the whole picture of a particular situation, and to advance the interests of the nation as a whole.[172]

NSCs are meeting forums for members of the executive branch of governments. They are not policy-making institutions. Especially in democracies, it should be kept in mind that NSC staff members are not elected officials and thus cannot replace the policy-making function of legislatures. Moreover, NSC meetings are usually held in secret. Keeping NSC membership small and tight makes it easier to ensure that national security deliberations at the cabinet level remain secret.[173] NSCs are there to advise the head of the executive branch of government on different policy options, and to monitor the implementation of national security policy. They are to ensure that the president or prime minister is made aware of the full range of options as well as the range of possible consequences of each policy option.

In their advisory role, NSCs can be said to be as influential as the president or prime minister allows them to be. Moreover, a state's constitution lays down the limits of presidential or prime ministerial powers when it comes to implementing security policy. In many countries, legislatures control the budget and thus have a say in determining which policy option receives the funding necessary for it to be implemented. Constitutions often also specify the need for the approval of the legislature when it comes to sending troops abroad.

Yet NSCs have the unique advantage of not representing the points of view and interests of individual government departments or political factions. These advisory bodies can thus be more objective in their advice regarding the country's security-related priorities. Moreover, by bringing together various experts and heads of different government departments and agencies, NSCs are uniquely equipped to deal with complex security issues, which can no longer be assigned to individual departments to be resolved. An NSC is therefore able to coordinate different interests and interrelated security issues effectively.

1. The Model: The US National Security Council of 1947

The United States was the first country to formally establish an NSC in 1947.[174] The United States has the most sophisticated NSC system in place today, and it is thus worth studying the US model in detail.

In the United States, the NSC emerged out of a desire by both President Harry Truman and the US Congress to centralise the intelligence community and reorganise national security policy making after World War II. Reflecting on the surprise attack by the Japanese on 7 December 1941, and looking at the way key pieces of information that pointed to an impending Japanese attack were dispersed around different US government departments, Truman is reported to have said: "If we'd all had that information in one agency, by God, I believe we could have foreseen what was going to happen in Pearl Harbor".[175]

Against Truman's will, however, Congress sought to create a formal institution that formed an integral part of the executive branch and was tasked with evaluating and coordinating national security policy across the different government departments and agencies.[176] Congress hoped that setting up "formal interagency consultative structures" would help the president make more effective security policy decisions.[177] The NSC was established by the 1947 National Security Act. Although President Truman welcomed the idea of having an experienced group of security policy advisers on hand, he did not want the NSC to assume any decision-making function.

The start of the Korean War in 1950 served as the impetus for President Truman to get the NSC much more involved in policy making. As one account of the period recalls: "Truman's increased use of the NSC system brought about procedures that have endured to the present day, including interagency committees with responsibilities for specific regional and functional areas, analysis and development of policy options, and recommendations for Presidential decisions."[178] Each subsequent US President has adapted the NSC to serve his particular style and meet his particular needs.

The President's National Security Adviser is responsible for the day-to-day management of the country's security affairs but is not a statutory member of the NSC, although today he forms an integral part of the council.[179] For example, President George W. Bush lets his National Security Adviser preside over NSC meetings in his absence. In the United States, the National Security Adviser serves a key function in security policy making because she or he sets the agenda for the NSC meetings in consultation with the statutory members of the NSC.[180] Because the National Security Adviser is not attached to any government department, he or she is free of departmental responsibilities and biases.[181]

Today, the US NSC is headed by a core group of about six senior presidential security policy advisers. This core group, also referred to as the Principals Committee, consists of the Secretaries of State, Defense and Treasury, the National Security Adviser, the Director of National Intelligence and the Chairman of the Joint Chiefs of Staff. Depending on the President, his Chief of Staff and Vice President regularly take part in the meetings of the Principals Committee.[182] Other senior officials might be asked to attend these meetings as well, depending on the issue being discussed.

Subordinated to the Principals Committee is the Deputies Committee, which is "composed of the deputy or relevant under secretaries to the cabinet secretaries".[183] As one report observes, "Historically, the [Deputies Committee] is where the bulk of the government's policy decisions are made in preparation for the [Principals Committee's] review and the President's decision".[184]

The Deputies Committee is assisted by an ever-growing staff of experts, political appointees, members of the different government departments and military officers working on substantive policy issues and managing national security affairs for the President on a daily basis.[185] The staff is dispersed among a number of regional and functional interagency working groups called Policy Coordination Committees (PCCs).[186] The PCCs are tasked with drafting analyses and policy proposals to submit to more senior NSC committees.[187] The NSC today has over 200 staff members.

As is mentioned above, an NSC is to a certain degree only as powerful as a country's leader is willing to allow it to be by including it in policy making. US President Ronald Reagan, for example, believed that the NSC policy recommendations should not subdue the policy initiatives of different government departments. As a consequence, he made his National Security Adviser, who headed the NSC, report to his Chief of Staff rather than to himself.[188]

Today, however, the NSC in the United States is being accused by some of having too much power over the security policy-making process. Some have noted that the NSC has become more like an agency involved in the details of day-to-day policy making instead of remaining an advisory body focused on important long-term security-related threats and trends.[189] It has turned into a large bureaucratic structure advancing its own perspective on the country's security challenges. As Ivo Daalder and I.M. Destler note, "With its own press, legislative, communication, and speechmaking offices, the NSC today conducts ongoing relations with the media, Congress, the American public, and foreign governments."[190] Similarly, the US Commission on National Security/21st Century warned in a January 2001 report that "Assuming a central policymaking role seriously detracts from the NSC staff's primary roles of honest broker and policy coordinator".[191]

(a) The US Homeland Security Council

Following the terrorist attacks of 11 September 2001, the US government established a Homeland Security Council (HSC), responsible for coordinating policies related to homeland security.[192] It deals with the defence of the homeland from internal threats and attacks and the securing of US borders. While national security deals with security threats that come from outside the country, homeland security deals with internal security threats. In practice, however, the two areas are deeply intertwined.

The HSC system is closely modelled on the NSC system. Some areas of research and policy making in the two councils, of course, overlap. However, most of the members of the NSC Principals Committee also serve on the HSC, and the National Security Adviser is invited to attend all HSC meetings.[193] NSC and HSC areas of responsibility are usually divided up and coordinated at the Deputies Committee level of the two agencies.[194]

2. Comparison of Select NSCs Around the World

After the United States established its NSC, several other countries created their own council. Each country has adapted its security council in its own way, especially in accordance with its particular system of government. Table 1 shows the composition of NSCs in several key states. The table compares the defined function of the NSC in each country, who chairs the meetings of the NSC core group, which government representatives are present, how the military is represented and which additional members regularly attend meetings of the NSC core group.

Table 1: Comparison of Select National Security Council Core Groups Around the World

Country (date NSC created)	Function	Chair	Government representatives	Military representative	Additional members
United States (1947)[1]	Limited advisory role; at request of the President, provides analyses of military and security policies, drafts policy options, makes recommendations for Presidential decisions.	**President**[2]	**- Vice President** **- Secretary of State** **- Secretary of Defense** - Secretary of the Treasury	**Chairman of the Joint Chiefs of Staff** *(rank of General)*	- National Security Adviser - Chief of Staff to the President - Assistant to the President for Economic Policy - Assistant to the President for Homeland Security - Counsel to the President - **Director of National Intelligence** - Attorney General and Director of the Office of Management and Budget on invitation **[Total of 12 members or more]**

[1] A.G. Whittaker, F.C. Smith, E. McKune, "The National Security Policy Process: The National Security Council and Interagency System," Research Report, August 2005 Annual Update, Industrial College of the Armed Forces, National Defense University, U.S. Department of Defense, accessed 20 February 2007, http://www.ndu.edu/icaf/; "National Security Council," The White House, President George W. Bush, accessed on 4 June 2007, http://www.whitehouse.gov/nsc.

[2] Statutory members in bold (remaining members regularly attend official meetings of the current US NSC)

Country (date NSC created)	Function	Chair	Government representatives	Military representative	Additional members
South Korea[3] (1948)	Advises the President on security issues.	President	- Prime Minister - Director of the Agency for National Security Planning - Ministers of Defense, Foreign Affairs, Home Affairs, Finance		**[Total of 7 members]**
Turkey (1962)	Give advice to the cabinet; Constitution asks the cabinet to give NSC advice "priority consideration". National Security Council Law of 1983 defines national security broadly as including "the defence and protection of the state against every kind of external and internal threat to the constitutional order, national existence, unity, and to all its interests and contractual rights in the international arena, including in the political, social, cultural and economic spheres".[4]	President	- Prime Minister - Chief of Staff - Minister of Defence - Minister of Interior - Foreign Minister	Commanders of - Army - Navy - Air Force	**[Total of approx. 9 members]**

[3] "South Korea – Constitution," accessed on 3 December 2007, http://www.servat.unibe.ch/law/icl/ks00000_.html; "National Security Council," Intelligence Resource Program, Federation of American Scientists, 18 July 1999, http://www.fas.org/irp/world/rok/nsc.htm.

[4] H.A. Rizvi, "National Security Council: A Comparative Study of Pakistan and Other Selected Countries," Pildat Background Paper, August 2005, http://fes.org.pk/publications/969-558-015-7.pdf, p. 11.

Country (date NSC created)	Function	Chair	Government representatives	Military representative	Additional members
Japan (1986)[5]	Advises on a wide range of military and non-military security issues.	Prime Minister	- Foreign Minister - Finance Minister - Chief cabinet secretary - Director General, Economic Planning Agency - Chairman, National Public Safety Commission		Invited state ministers or officials **[Total of at least 6 members]**
Russia (1992)	"Drafts policy proposals on defending the vital interests of individuals, society and the state against internal and external threats...[It] also helps determine a uniform state policy on security and helps ensure the President's ability to carry out his constitutional duties in defending human and civil rights, as well as Russia's sovereignty, independence and territorial integrity".[6]	President	*No information found*	*No information found*	Assisted by Scholarly Council made up of academics and experts

[5] "Security Council," Intelligence Resource Program, Federation of American Scientists, 12 October 2000, http://www.fas.org/irp/world/japan/sc.htm.

[6] "The Security Council," President of Russia Official Web Portal, accessed on 20 February 2007, http://www.kremlin.ru/eng/print/institut04.shtml.

Country (date NSC created)	Function	Chair	Government representatives	Military representative	Additional members
Iran[7] (1997)	Formulates defence and national security policies according to the guidelines by the Supreme Leader; coordinates security policies and the country's politics, social, cultural, and economic fields, and intelligence; mobilises material and intellectual resources to address internal and external threats. *Decisions become effective upon confirmation by the Supreme Leader.*	President	Heads of the - Executive - Legislative - Judiciary; Minister of Foreign Affairs; Minister of the Interior	- Chief of the Supreme Command Council of the Armed Forces; - highest ranking officer of the Armed Forces; - Commander of Islamic Revolutionary Guards	- 2 representatives appointed by the Leader - official in charge of the Plan on Budget Organisation **[Total of 12 members]**
India (1998)[8]	- Limited advisory role on "external and internal security, military affairs, conventional and non-conventional defence, space and high technology, counter-insurgency, counter-terrorism, economy, environment".[9] - Heads Strategic Planning Group and National Security Advisory Board.	Prime Minister	Union Minister of - Home - Defense - External Affairs - Finance; Deputy Chairman of the Planning Commission	***No*** *military representative in NSC apex body; Services chiefs part of second-tier Strategic Planning Group*	- National Security Adviser - invited cabinet members and senior officials **[Total of 7 members or more]**

[7] "Supreme Defense Council (SDC)," GlobalSecurity.org, accessed on 14 May 2007, http://www.globalsecurity.org/military/world/iran/sdc.htm; Rizvi, *op. cit.*, note 3, p. 11.

[8] Rizvi, *op. cit.*, note 3, p. 10.

Country (date NSC created)	Function	Chair	Government representatives	Military representative	Additional members
Israel (1999)[10]	Provide information and make recommend-ations on national security issues to the Prime Minister and the Cabinet; coordination of national security policy; long-term planning of national security.	Council Chairman/ National Security Adviser (*appointed by Prime Minister*)	Heads of Division for: - Security Policy - Foreign Policy - Company and Infrastructure Policy - Terror Combat		- Economic Adviser - Legal Adviser **[Total of 7 members]**
Pakistan (2004)[11]	- Serves as a "forum for consultation to the President and the government on matters of national security including the sovereignty, integrity, defence, security of the state and crisis management".[12] - Formulates and recommends policy options.	President	- Prime Minister - Senate Chairman - Speaker, National Assembly - Opposition leader, National Assembly	- Chairman, Joint Chiefs of Staff Committee - Heads of the Navy, Army and Air Force	- Chief Ministers of all 4 Pakistani provinces - Cabinet members, other government officials and outside experts on invitation **[Total of 13 members or more]**

[9] *Ibid.*
[10] *Ibid.,* p. 12; "National Security Council," Prime Minister's Office, Government of Israel, accessed 20 February 2007, http://www.pmo.gov.il.
[11] Rizvi, *op. cit*., note 3, pp. 15-16.
[12] *Ibid.,* p. 16.

Country (date NSC created)	Function	Chair	Government representatives	Military representative	Additional members
The Three Pillar Model of Sustainable National Security in a Trans-national World (this book, © N.R.F. Al-Rodhan 2008)[13]	Advises the head of state on a broad range of security issues and acts as an honest broker between the security interests of individual government departments; drafts analyses of potential future security threats; monitors inter-national events and brings security concerns to the attention of the government.	Head of State/ National Security Adviser	Head of State; Deputy Head of State; Heads of - Foreign - Defence - Treasury - Economics Departments; Homeland Security Adviser; Economics Adviser; Director of National Intelligence	Chairman of the Joint Chiefs of Staff	- Chiefs of 10 Issue Groups - Chiefs of 8 Principles and Future Trajectories Divisions **[Total of approx. 29 members, depending on the size and specific security needs of individual countries]**

The Three Pillar Model of Sustainable National Security in a Transnational World is discussed in more detail in chapter 6. It is meant to be an ideal comprehensive structure that addresses every aspect of national security. However, it is up to every state to adapt the model to fit its particular needs.

As Table 1 illustrates, most NSCs are chaired directly by the president or prime minister of a particular country. The executive is in most cases represented by the heads of several key departments, including the foreign, economic and defence ministries. As the discussion below demonstrates in more detail, it is interesting to observe the way in which the government structures of each state are reflected in the composition of each NSC.

(a) The Position of a National Security Adviser

The person who heads the NSC meetings will have an influence on the kinds of threats that NSC policy recommendations focus on. In the United States, although the President chairs the NSC, it is often the President's hand-picked National Security Adviser who leads and, in the President's absence, sometimes even chairs the NSC meetings.

---

[13] N.R.F. Al-Rodhan, *The Three Pillars of* Sustainable National Security *in a Transnational World* (Berlin: LIT Verlag, 2008), this book.

This gives the National Security Adviser a powerful role in security council deliberations. His or her intellectual and professional background can as a result strongly influence the topics that are discussed and the policy options that are favoured by the NSC. As one scholar notes, National Security Advisers in the United States have never been experts in the areas of economics, internal security and intelligence gathering, so US NSCs "tended to over-focus on foreign policy matters" and thus did not pay enough attention to threats related to internal security, especially terrorism.[195]

The advantage of having a National Security Adviser as a permanent member of the NSC is that this person is able to concentrate fully on national security policy making and is thus not tied up with other government responsibilities. In systems where a National Security Adviser runs NSC meetings, it is important that a president or prime minister chooses somebody he or she can fully trust. As is shown in the comparisons table, a majority of presidents and prime ministers chair their NSC in person whenever possible. Israel might be an exception here, as the National Security Adviser usually chairs the NSC meetings on behalf of the prime minister. Among the NSCs compared in the table, India is the only other country with a National Security Adviser among its permanent NSC members.

(b) The Positioning of the NSC in a Country's Political System

The composition of the NSC can in many ways reflect the power structure of a state's political system.[196] In established democracies, where the military does not form part of the government, the military leadership will play a similarly subordinated role in national security policy making.[197] This is different in countries where the military has traditionally had a prominent role in governance. In these cases, "the NSC provides the military top brass with a constitutional and legal umbrella to stay engaged in policy making and monitoring of the civilian or semi-civilian government in a discreet manner. This gives them an additional leverage and the NSC tends to become [a] policy setting and supervisory body."[198]

Turkey is a case in point where the military has had a strong role in the country's political history. The military sees itself not just as the guardian of the state as a physical entity, but also as the guarantor of Turkey's republican and secular political system.[199] The military is well represented on the NSC, which allows it to influence policy making and keep a close eye on the government's handling of security affairs.[200] In the light of its candidacy for EU membership, Turkey has implemented a series of democratic reforms in the past few years which limit the military's influence in politics. This has also been reflected in the NSC where, in 2004, the president for the first time appointed a civilian Secretary General of the NSC (former Turkish Ambassador to Greece Yigit Alpogan), rather than, as in the past, a four-star general.[201]

In the case of Iran, every decision of the Supreme Council for National Security (SCNS) requires the approval of the country's Supreme Leader, a clergyman, before it is implemented.[202]

(c) The Role of the Armed Forces

It is interesting to compare the level of participation of the military in different NSC models. The way the military is represented in a country's NSC says a lot about its status and its influence on policy making.

In India, for example, the armed forces are not represented in the apex body of the NSC and thus are divorced from the national security decision-making processes.[203] The Service Chiefs are only members of the second-tier Strategic Planning Group, where the majority of members are the secretaries of state of the federal ministries.[204]

The reason for this strict separation can be traced back to early post-independence India. At the time, Prime Minister Jawaharlal Nehru sought to keep the Indian armed forces separate from national security policy making because he feared that India might otherwise share the fate of other, newly independent, states, which had become military dictatorships. India's civilian bureaucrats supported Nehru's strategy because it allowed them to remain the only elite with direct access to the political leadership.[205]

In Pakistan, by contrast, the military leadership soon came to occupy a key role in security policy making after independence. At the time of independence, the country faced a series of external security threats and the territorial integrity and survival of the state became the highest priority for policy makers. Hence, the state depended on a strong military.[206]

In the United States, the Chairman of the Joint Chiefs of Staff of the Armed Forces serves as the statutory military adviser to the NSC core group. The latter is the only uniformed member of the US NSC. Although his presence does provide "an institutionalised link"[207] between the civilian leadership and the military, and thus allows the military to be involved in strategic planning in time of war and peace, the military role is clearly subordinate to the civil.[208]

In Pakistan, those supporting the active participation of the military in NSC deliberations argue that well-coordinated policy making between the military and civilian branches of government helps to promote political stability.[209] Moreover, supporters argue that it provides a check on the powers of the president – who until recently also was head of the Armed Forces – and thus on the military.[210] In other words, this line of argument maintains that the inclusion of the military top brass in this important civilian institution has a moderating effect on the military.

In contrast, opponents of the creation of an NSC in Pakistan argue that the NSC will strengthen the presidency and with it the top military commanders at the expense of the elected parliament. Since its formal creation in 2004, Pakistan's NSC has covered a broad range of topics in its discussions. As one analyst observed at the time, "As the President is concurrently holding the office of the Chief of Army Staff, the NSC is a policy setting institution rather than making policy recommendations to the federal cabinet."[211]

The case of Turkey may partly support the argument that giving the military a stronger voice in the political decision-making process does not shield a civilian government from a military coup. In Turkey, the military has taken power in a coup in the past, and time and again threatens to do so – despite being well-represented in the Turkish NSC.

(d) Additional NSC Members

As is clear from table 1, the number of permanent NSC members differs from state to state. Surprisingly, almost none of the NSC boards compared in the table seems to have a representative of the intelligence community on staff. The United States, where the Director of National Intelligence is a constitutional member of the NSC, is the exception.

In Russia, what stands out is the inclusion of academic experts from a Scholarly Council in NSC deliberations. According to the official Russian Presidential website, the Scholarly Council consists of "representatives of the Russian Academy of Sciences, specialized academies of science and educational institutions, as well as other academics and experts".[212]

Pakistan is the only state that has representatives of the country's different regions on the NSC. These representatives are to ensure that the interests of all four Pakistani provinces are taken into account in security policy deliberations.

3. National Security Decision-making Structures in Countries without an NSC: The Examples of the United Kingdom and France

Political systems with a president but no prime minister, such as the US system, have a special need for an office that coordinates policy between the different departments. The US model contrasts with parliamentary democracies that have a prime minister. In these cases, the prime minister and his or her cabinet take on the role of consolidating and unifying national policy and taking inter-ministerial decisions. This section examines two major European countries – the United Kingdom and France – which have until now made security policy without a distinct advisory body in the form of an NSC.

(a) The United Kingdom

In the United Kingdom, coordination of security policy rests with the Cabinet Office. Prior to the events of 11 September 2001, the Cabinet Secretary coordinated national security policy between the intelligence agencies, civilian ministries and the military. He was assisted by the Chairman of the Joint Intelligence Committee (JIC), responsible for the assessment of the intelligence provided by the different agencies and the coordination of physical security. Actual formulation and implementation of foreign and defence policies, however, rested with the heads of the Foreign Office and the Defence Department.[213]

In 2002, the British Prime Minister, Tony Blair, created a new Cabinet Office position, that of Security and Intelligence Coordinator and Permanent Secretary, to take over the responsibilities related to security and intelligence from the Cabinet Secretary. The Security and Intelligence Coordinator is tasked with intelligence coordination, internal security, crisis management and disaster management. The new post still reports to the Cabinet Secretary – and thus only indirectly to the Prime Minister – and is assisted by the staff of the Cabinet Office. Concerning foreign and defence policy, the Prime Minister is advised by his personal adviser on foreign policy. Implementation and formulation of foreign policy, however, continues to rest with the Foreign Office.[214]

National security matters in the UK thus are handled by three senior officials under the direction of the Prime Minister: the adviser on foreign policy; the Security and Intelligence Coordinator; and the Chairman of the Joint Intelligence Committee, who is assisted by the staff of the Joint Intelligence Organisation in assessing intelligence.[215]

Several characteristics stand out when looking at the British model. First, the British national security structure is not rigidly institutionalised and thus remains quite flexible. Second, the Cabinet Secretary stands at the centre of the national security mechanism and oversees the whole process. At the same time, formulation and implementation of national security-related policies rests with the departments that deal with the policy areas concerned. Moreover, the heads of the different intelligence agencies remain under the administrative control of their respective departments, that is, the Security Service (MI5) as part of the Home Office and the Secret Intelligence Service (MI6) as part of the Foreign Office.[216] The Cabinet Office committee system, which brings together all the government departments concerned with a particular security threat, has proved very effective at coordinating security policy. In particular, the system is able quickly to analyse and act on terrorist-related intelligence. While the system is highly effective at taking short-term decisions and responding to imminent threats, however, its ability to develop long-term security strategies is rather poor. Hence, different policy responses to different threats at home and abroad are often not in line with each other, and the different policy responses do not necessarily contribute to an overarching national security doctrine.[217]

Following the attempted car bombings in London and Glasgow during the first few days of the administration of Prime Minister Gordon Brown in 2007, Brown announced the creation of a National Security Council by the British Government. The NSC, Brown stated, would regularly publish a national security strategy and send out "a clear message" of vigilance.[218] Headed by the Prime Minister, it will include key ministers and, whenever appropriate, the UK's defence chief and the heads of the country's intelligence services.[219] The council would thus replace several Cabinet committees that deal with terrorism and security issues. According to Brown, its task would be to "coordinate military, policing, intelligence and diplomatic action and also to win hearts and minds in this country and around the world".[220]

The latter, additional, task – to communicate British national security policy to its citizens and the international community in order to win their support – is particularly noteworthy. As is explained in more detail below, good communication is a crucial aspect of national security policy making in the 21st century.

(b) France

France has a presidential system, whereby the president has extensive powers in foreign and defence policy matters. Interestingly, the concept of "national" security does not exist in France. Instead, the French think in terms of domestic security and international security. The intelligence community is also split accordingly between the Directorate of the External Security (DGSE), on the one hand, and domestic intelligence, on the other – the latter being part of the Ministry of the Interior.

France has a director general of political affairs and security within the Ministry of Foreign Affairs. The directorate defines security as "safeguarding the international order guaranteeing peace, but also defending against the new threats of, for example, terrorism".[221] The directorate is divided into four different branches or areas of responsibility. First, the department of the United Nations and International Organisations (NUOI) "defines and implements France's actions in international organisations and inter-governmental organisations".[222] It also makes sure that binding resolutions passed by the UN Security Council and other international bodies of which France is a member are properly implemented by French missions.[223] Second, the department of strategic affairs, security and disarmament is concerned with the non-proliferation and eventual disarmament of nuclear, chemical and biological weapons; conventional security and defence issues; and some newer issues such as the fight against terrorism, drug trafficking and international crime.[224] A third department is concerned with "military and defence co-operation with all foreign states".[225] The fourth department is responsible for the CFSP, adopted by EU member states on signing the Maastricht Treaty in 1992.[226] It prepares for official meetings held on the topic by EU member states.[227]

France's domestic security has been threatened by foreign-inspired terrorist attacks since the 1950s, and the country was hit by an unprecedented terror wave in the mid-1980s. France's security apparatus reacted to the new menace by forming a close relationship between the judiciary and the domestic intelligence service. In France, members of the domestic intelligence service are empowered to ask magistrates to start an investigation. Moreover, judges can support the intelligence service by authorising warrants, wiretaps and subpoenas.[228] France deals with the terrorist menace by focusing on "aggressive prosecution, specialised investigators, and intrusive law enforcement".[229] The level of cooperation between the two branches is unique in the Western world. The French system allows for a high level of intrusiveness on the part of the police, and civil liberties may on some occasions be violated as a result; yet this is a trade-off the French people seem willing to accept when it comes to domestic security.[230]

France is currently considering the establishment of an NSC-like body – composed mainly of diplomats – working under the direction of the president. It is most likely that the main consequence of such a new body would be the strengthening of the president's office, while the ministry of foreign affairs would be deprived of some of its most experienced diplomats. In other words, power in the security policy sector, especially external security, would shift from the department of foreign affairs to the presidency. The French President, Nicolas Sarkozy, has established a commission to work out a new national defence and security policy by the beginning of 2008, which takes account of the new security environment and establishes new procedures that allow France to take "decisive decisions" to ensure its continued security.[231]

4. Governance and Control of Nuclear Weapons

The question of how to handle the procurement, development, maintenance and potential use of nuclear weapons is a key national security issue for all declared and de facto nuclear weapon states. How much decision-making power should the head of the civilian executive, the military, and perhaps even the legislature, respectively, have over these weapons – the deployment of which will inevitably have the most severe humanitarian, ethical and geopolitical consequences? How do countries try to avoid the accidental release of a nuclear device? And how can states protect nuclear weapons from theft by third parties? These are some of the questions every state that possesses these weapons has to grapple with within their national security structure.

There are five declared nuclear weapon states, which are officially recognised as such in the Nuclear Non-Proliferation Treaty

(NPT), which entered into force in 1970. These states, which incidentally also constitute the five permanent members of the UN Security Council, are the United States, Russia, China, the UK and France. Israel, India and Pakistan are considered de facto nuclear weapon states, which means that they are not officially recognised as nuclear powers, are not parties to the NPT, but are believed to possess a nuclear weapon capability.[232]

The nuclear capabilities and strategies of the five established nuclear weapon states differ from each other. The United States and Russia are the only nuclear powers with nuclear arsenals large and sophisticated enough to give them first-strike and war-fighting capabilities. The other three nuclear weapon states have smaller arsenals and thus only second-strike capabilities to retaliate against an attack by another state. They do not maintain war-fighting capabilities. China has so far adopted a strict non-first-use policy, meaning that it would only use nuclear weapons in response to a nuclear attack. In contrast, the UK and France reserve the right to retaliate with nuclear weapons in the case of a conventional attack on their countries.[233]

In the United States, the first nuclear weapon state, only the president can authorise the deployment of nuclear weapons, while the military has physical custodianship. This chain of authority regarding the launch of a nuclear weapon is supported by a system of permissive action links (PALs), whereby the president is in possession of a secret electronic code, without which the military is unable to release the weapons. Other safety measures are in place to protect the weapons from theft and accidental or unauthorised release.[234] Although the president has the final say on nuclear doctrine, development and operational status, the Office of the Secretary of Defense and the Joint Chiefs of Staff, along with the Department of State, the Department of Energy and the National Security Council, take part in the decision-making process regarding nuclear issues.[235] Since the president is also Commander-in-Chief of the armed forces, the president also has the final say in choosing the targets of a US nuclear attack. Congress indirectly keeps a limited check on the president's nuclear strategy by having the final say on approving defence spending, including spending earmarked for nuclear weapons development.[236] All in all, the US nuclear system is quite transparent and open, and nuclear issues are widely discussed among politicians, academics and other members of civil society.

The Russian Federation has inherited the large nuclear arsenal of the Soviet Union. Russia's huge nuclear capabilities allow the country to claim the status of a major military superpower, and the possession and development of these nuclear assets are no secret. However, nuclear decisions are made in secret by a small group of government officials.[237] The president makes decisions on the development (including funding), storage and deployment of nuclear weapons. However, he shares authority over the use of nuclear weapons with the defence minister and the chief of the general staff, because the release codes are controlled by the three of them together.[238] The Russian Parliament has little say over nuclear strategy.

In China, the third-largest nuclear weapon state, nuclear weapons are under the tight grip of the CCP. The CCP is therefore strongly connected with the military. In China, the General Secretary of the CCP usually also serves as the country's president and military chief. Hence, the General Secretary also presides over "the two top decision-making bodies for defence policy – the Politburo Standing Committee (PBSC) and the Central Military Commission (CMC)", both members of the CCP.[239] Decisions about nuclear weapons are made collectively by the leadership of these bodies, which directly controls the military's execution of its orders.[240] China is also believed to have a PALs system in place.[241] Chinese nuclear issues are handled in conditions of the utmost secrecy.

In France, the president has traditionally had strong powers in the areas of foreign and defence policy. The French President also has control over the deployment of nuclear weapons, including their status of alert. The president is in possession of the enabling codes of every nuclear missile in the French military.[242] According to Hans Born, "Decisions concerning the use of nuclear weapons would generally involve only three people: the president, the chief of the presidential military staff and the chief of the defence staff."[243] Following a 1964 presidential decree, the French Parliament has no role in decisions concerning nuclear weapons.

In the UK, decisions over the development of nuclear strategy, nuclear weapons and their use are taken by the prime minister and his or her Cabinet. Following a prime ministerial order, British nuclear missiles can only be launched by turning several keys, each held by a different officer.[244] The British Parliament, by convention, does not exercise its power of veto over the budget when it comes to defence spending. Its role in decisions regarding nuclear policy is more one of questioning government policy on the issue.[245] As well as its own limited nuclear arsenal, the UK also has US nuclear weapons on its territory as part of NATO policy. Although the United States retains full control over these weapons, it is assumed that the United States would consult the British Government before launching them.[246]

Israel is believed to have somewhere between 100 and 300 nuclear warheads, although it has officially neither confirmed nor denied its possession of nuclear weapons.[247] It is believed that the prime minister directly controls nuclear issues, together with a few other civilian executive officials: "Internal advisory panels of economists, chief scientists, army officers and academics with top security clearance are thought to exist, but information about such panels is not public".[248] Moreover, Israel is believed to have some sort of PALs system in place to protect the weapons. Because of the secrecy of the programme, the Israeli Parliament has no real role in decisions involving nuclear weapons. Israel is not a party to the NPT.[249]

Since its successful underground nuclear weapon tests in 1998, India has become a de facto nuclear weapon state. The country has been working on a nuclear doctrine, which is based on a policy of no-first-use. It is believed that the country keeps its nuclear warheads separate from their delivery vehicles.[250] India's nuclear weapons are governed by three entities: "The scientific establishment holds the nuclear warheads, the military holds the delivery systems and the political authorities exercise general oversight inter alia of weapon use".[251] The military is thus kept in check and prevented from acting on its own. In 2003, the Indian Government established a Nuclear Command Authority to manage the country's nuclear weapons, which is made up of the Executive Council, headed by the national security adviser, and the Political Council, headed by the prime minister. Only the Political Council can order the use of nuclear weapons. The order from the Political Council would then be passed to the Strategic Forces Command, which controls India's nuclear forces.[252] Parliament has so far had no significant role in decisions involving nuclear weapons. The country's defence budget does not disclose the funds allocated to the nuclear programme.[253] To help India secure its nuclear arsenals, the United States is negotiating an agreement with India on nuclear cooperation, through which the United States would provide nuclear technological assistance in exchange for India assuming "the same responsibilities and practices" as the official nuclear weapon states.[254] This entails "distinguishing India's military facilities from civilian ones and putting all civilian facilities under International Atomic Energy Agency (IAEA) safeguards".[255] The deal, which has not yet been ratified, is highly controversial, as critics point out that the United States should not reward nuclear weapon proliferation.

Pakistan has been a de facto nuclear weapon state since its nuclear tests in 1998. In 2000, the country's military government handed control of development, strategy and deployment of nuclear weapons to the newly created National Command Authority (NCA). Chaired by the president, the NCA has both civilian and military members, although the military representatives are in a clear majority. The use of nuclear weapons must be authorised unanimously by three officials: the president, the prime minister and a third, unidentified, person. Parliament has so far had no say in the nuclear issue.[256] The United States and other countries have repeatedly expressed concern about the safety of Pakistan's nuclear weapons – not just from theft but, more importantly, from a scenario whereby the current government is overthrown by extremists who might be more ready to use the weapons. The United States has allegedly provided Pakistan with PALs and other security devices to protect its nuclear weapons.[257]

Countries are using a broad range of mechanisms to ensure the safety of their borders and their people. National security councils can form an important component in a country's security structure. They serve as a neutral platform where the heads of different government departments can discuss and coordinate their security-related concerns and come up with appropriate policy recommendations. A properly functioning NSC has the ability to ensure that a state's security policy does not become dominated or monopolised by a single government department but takes into account a variety of security-related issues affecting the state. National security councils so far have been more common in presidential systems that lack a cabinet where senior policy makers meet regularly to take decisions. Presidential systems thus have a particularly urgent need to coordinate the policies of different government departments and act as a platform where the heads of these departments can meet and coordinate the most crucial aspects of a country's policy agenda – ensuring the survival of the state and the safety of its citizens. Yet, as current discussions in France and Britain suggest, even political systems with a prime minister, whose cabinet usually takes up a central coordinating function in the government, are considering the establishment of a unified institutionalised setting where security policy can be drafted and long-term strategy be discussed. NSC-like structures are important for any state that wants to make effective national security policy in the 21st century. Before making a proposal for a new style NSC, however, this study discusses the plethora of security threats that states face today.

CHAPTER 4

CHALLENGES TO NATIONAL SECURITY IN AN INSTANT AND INTERDEPENDENT WORLD

States in the early 21st century face threats that are either “new” or have become intensified due to the advent of economic globalisation and the development of new technologies, ranging from information technology to biotechnology. Other new threats are connected to demographic developments and environmental issues. The security landscape is certainly changing, and officials tasked with protecting the national security of states will have to shift their attention to incorporate non-military threats into their national security strategies.

One author suggests that a significant change in the post-Cold War security environment is the increased focus on poor and unstable states as the locus and source of security threats.[258] Countries stricken by pervasive poverty and political instability are the location for the majority of violent conflicts today, which is in fact not so different from the Cold War period. More significantly, perhaps, poor and unstable states are also the main source of many non-traditional or new threats to the security of states, as is discussed below. This chapter demonstrates that chronic economic underdevelopment and low living standards can be a factor in state failure – which entails a state’s inability to effectively address a variety of threats affecting other states, including the spread of disease and organised crime, and mass migration.

This chapter provides an overview of the variety of threats that states face today. It will become clear from the discussion below that security policy making now requires the expertise of a broad range of experts, ranging from experts on the environment and human health to computer technology. Some of the threats discussed below are interrelated, which leads to the conclusion that strong cooperation among the various experts is a prerequisite for effective security policy making.

1. Changing Global Power Structures, State Failure and Regional Conflicts

Geopolitical issues, involving a combination of political, economic, demographic and geographic factors determining power relationships among states, will remain on the security policy agenda of states in the 21st century. Yet, increased global interconnectedness and economic globalisation have modified the parameters of traditional power politics. Globalisation has changed the power relationships between states. Economic clout today weighs much more heavily when measuring the relative power and influence of a state in international politics than it used to. States are also increasingly worried about what might be called "weak links" in the international state system. These weak links are states that are either unable or unwilling to cooperate with other states in dealing with a variety of security issues, such as weapons proliferation or the spread of infectious diseases. Failed states, for example, do not pose a threat to the international state system because they seek to alter state borders or conquer new territory. They pose a threat because the inability of these states to control their own territory has security implications for neighbours in the region and the world as a whole. This section deals with issues related to the stability of today's international system of states.

(a) Changing Global Power Structures

The process of globalisation is likely to precipitate changes in the global balance of power. Some analysts believe that since globalisation disproportionately benefits developed states with a capitalist economy and a democratic form of government, these states will grow even more dominant in the next few decades. As the global market economy promotes mainly Western trade norms and Western cultural values, it benefits those states that already embrace them.[259]

In this context, Jonathan Kirshner expects that today's dominant world power, the United States, will become even more pre-eminent in the next decades. According to Kirshner, the United States' "advantages in world finance, information dominance, cultural position and appeal, and the size, attractiveness, and adaptability of its home market" will ensure the continuation, even enhancement, of its global dominance.[260] Moreover, as a world leader in information and communication technology (ICT), the United States is likely to continue or enhance its military predominance due to its ability to apply ICT for military purposes.

That said, however, Kirshner cautions that US global dominance also makes it more exposed and vulnerable. The globalisation of finance has put the United States at increased risk of a financial crisis.[261] US preponderance also triggers more resistance to its strong cultural influence, economic dominance and military might.[262] Resistance may be at times political – coming, for example, from otherwise friendly governments unwilling to compromise on their own national interests to bend to US requests.[263] At other times, resistance may be violent, and may come from groups and individuals that oppose one or other aspect of what the United States stands for – be it its global military presence or the global economy.

Moreover, states where the economy is not developed enough to provide attractive jobs for skilled workers continue to be at risk of losing their best educated people to more developed states due to increased labour mobility. This does not bode well for the advancement of these states.[264]

Globalisation changes power relationships between states. Economic might is becoming more important than the size of a country's population or army. Economic globalisation possibly even reduces the incentives for territorial conquest among developed states. As Stephen G. Brooks argues, multinational corporations (MNCs), which benefit greatly from the globalised economic environment, today dominate global commerce. MNCs are not territorially constrained. They may conduct research and development in one country, production of components in another and assembly in a third. They rely on international subcontracting and outsourcing, and form alliances with other companies.[265] The global interdependence of MNCs ultimately has an effect on security relations between states, argues Brooks, at least among developed states. First, countries today are no longer self-sufficient when it comes to weapons production. If a country wants to keep its military capabilities up to date, it relies on other countries to provide components and technical know-how. Hence, argues Brooks, revisionist states may be more reluctant to "go it alone" for fear of an international embargo and losing access to necessary weapons technology.[266]

Second, conquest of territory has become much less attractive from an economic point of view than it used to be, for example, for Nazi Germany in World War II.[267] As MNCs have globalised their production, the wealth produced by these companies cannot be tapped by conquering a particular piece of territory on which part of their production process takes place. Moreover, as states depend so heavily on foreign capital for their economic well-being, territories conquered by a foreign power are unlikely to attract foreign investment.[268] Moreover, imperial control of a technologically advanced country will greatly undermine technological innovation, which is so important in today's knowledge-based economy.[269] Third, Brooks observes, states increasingly see it as in their interests to cooperate with other states to facilitate economic transactions and work towards regional economic integration. Stronger economic interdependence often translates into more peaceful security relationships.[270]

(b) Failed States as Regional and International Security Challenges

The problem of state failure has taken a prominent position in today's international security debate. A state is considered "failed" if the central government is no longer able to control its entire territory, promote law and order and provide basic public services to its population. States dubbed "weak" or "failing" are states that only partly succeed in fulfilling basic state functions and may be at risk of failing at some point. Both weak and failed states can cause serious spillover effects that threaten the national security of other states.

Many threats identified below accompany state failure, ranging from the spread of diseases to mass migration to violent conflict and organised crime. These security challenges can be either a cause or a consequence of the breakdown of law and order within a state.

The existence of "weak links" in the international system caused by the presence of ungoverned territories poses a threat to the global order and undermines international efforts to effectively tackle transnational security threats. Individual states can only be secure if the global order they are part of is somewhat predictable. Their economic well-being depends on the reliability of the international economic system. A "weak link" in the system can interrupt trade and transport flows and may provide safe havens for international criminal groups or terrorists. In short, states today, if they want to rest secure, depend on the ability of other states to be in control of their territory.

(c) 'Rogue' Nations

In 1994, Anthony Lake, President Clinton's national security adviser at the time, warned that states such as Cuba, North Korea and Iran constituted a particular type of states that posed a distinct set of security challenges to the international community. Lake referred to this type of state as "backlash states", which are today more commonly known as "rogue states". Lake identified a set of characteristics that these backlash states tend to share in common. Domestically, leaders of these states hold a tight grip on their society while suppressing any form of popular political participation. In international politics, their posture is aggressive and defiant. They are unwilling to submit to any kind of international norms and take on the role of international outsiders. According to Lake, these states feel that they are constantly under siege. As a consequence, they maintain large armies and spend a lot of money on weapons technology, including ambitious WMD programmes, to deter other nations and/or engage in adventurous policies themselves.[271]

Some scholars argue that rogue states pose a particularly difficult problem with regard to the proliferation of lethal weapons. Less integrated in the global order, rogue states "have a smaller stake in global stability" than others.[272] Their weakness and lack of reliable allies thus motivates them to "develop offensive postures by relying on the perceived power of unconventional arsenals".[273] WMD in the 21st century are at risk of evolving into a "'poor man's' source of influence"[274] – a powerful bargaining chip for some of these states. Moreover, there is the danger of rogue states passing on WMD to terrorists in defiance of the international community, out of a need for cash or due to their ideological allegiance to the cause espoused by a terrorist group.

(d) Ethnic, Tribal and Religious Warfare

A phenomenon of the post-World War II era has been the decline in the number of inter-state wars and the rise of intra-state wars. Donald M. Snow has also observed a shift in the nature of intra-state wars since the 1990s. To distinguish them from "regular" civil wars, he identifies the new type of wars that characterise the post-Cold War era as new internal wars (NIWs).[275] While civil wars are fought over the control of a central government, violent rebel groups in NIWs often have unclear or unspecified political objectives.[276] Sometimes, the goal of these warring parties is simply to create chaos and anarchy.

Their aim is to weaken the central government to such an extent that it cannot interfere with the pursuits of the rebel group, such as gaining control over precious resources or growing plants used for the production of illegal narcotics.[277] Snow writes that the real objective of these insurgencies "is to create a sense of total lawlessness that maximizes the group's ability to enrich itself either through thievery and worse or by controlling or protecting narcotics trafficking".[278]

The difference in the type of goals that warring parties pursue in NIWs has consequences for the way these wars are fought. Because warring parties in traditional civil wars vie for the control of the central government, it is in their interest to win over the "hearts and minds" of the civilian population in order to maximise popular support for their political cause. If successful, insurgents know that they will need to be able to rely on the long-term loyalty and support of a popular majority. This can be a barrier against excessive violence against non-combatants: "The need to appeal to the people thus moderates the violence".[279]

In contrast, insurgents in NIWs, who do not have aspirations to govern their country, tend not to shy away from using cruel and excessively violent tactics against their opponents. In the "absence of a shared center of gravity that needs to be nurtured…the purpose is to subdue, not to win over, the opponent".[280] In this sense, NIWs share similarities with interstate wars, where the goal is also to conquer and subdue the enemy, including the civilian population.[281] The lack of a clear strategy means that warring parties in NIWs "are typically highly irregular, not uniformed or organized into coherent rank orderings of officers and enlisted soldiers. They are poorly trained…and are unaware or contemptuous of normal conventions of war".[282]

Most NIWs are taking place at the periphery of the global economy and usually do not directly affect developed states. Yet, the conflicts often cannot be ignored by people and politicians in the developed world because of global television networks. Human suffering in countries affected by these wars is televised around the world and often causes an international outcry.[283]

The question of what states can or should do about these humanitarian crises has not been satisfactorily resolved. Because NIWs mostly occur in the poorest parts of the world, where people have little or nothing to lose, Snow concludes that "the prospects for NIWs…are as good as is the amount of suffering in the world".[284] Moreover, outside actors will continue to have great difficulty in creating peace in countries affected by NIWs, because warring parties often have no interest in creating any type of peace arrangement, not even one on their terms.[285] Nonetheless, allowing NIWs to continue is not in the interests of international peace and security, because NIWs, like ethnic conflicts, can cause instability in neighbouring states, and/or help to strengthen transnational organised crime.

2. The Security Implications of Population Growth, Migration and Refugee Flows

This section deals with a variety of demographic issues that affect the stability of states. It addresses the possible security implications of population growth, which today occurs mostly in the South, and migration patterns both within countries and across international borders.

(a) Population Growth

By 2050, some demographers predict that the world's population will have grown to 9-10 billion.[286] More than 95 percent of the population growth is predicted to be in poor countries, and Africa is expected to experience the largest amount of growth.[287] According to J.R. McNeill, a majority of the "next 3 billion will be born into circumstances of greater shortages of soil, water, and forests, and will see migration as their best option".[288] He therefore expects Europe to be the primary destination for migrants from Africa, which is likely to cause new points of friction.[289]

In the early stages of the modern era and into the 20th century, a state's population size was seen in relation to state power: the larger a state's population, the larger its industrial and military power.[290] In fact, the leading industrial powers at the beginning of the 20th century were also those with the largest population. Today, the world's population is distributed differently, with most of the population growth occurring in developing states. This new "imbalance" in the world's population ratios between the developed and developing world has not automatically translated into a reshuffling of the global balance of power in geopolitical terms.[291] The mass armies of the 19th and early 20th century have in some cases been replaced by nuclear weapons. Furthermore, economic strength and the mastery of sophisticated technology, including ICT, have become very important determining factors of a state's geopolitical status.[292]

Today, rapid population growth is often associated with state instability, political violence and mass migration. Rapid demographic changes can be a contributing factor to a number of internal and external security challenges.[293]

Rapid population growth almost naturally puts a strain on local resources – be it water and food supply, or public services such as healthcare facilities. Nevertheless, whether resource shortages ultimately lead to violent conflict depends on a country's particular socio-economic constellations. As Charles B. Keely observes, in situations where rapid population growth occurs in agricultural areas where the arable land is owned by a small elite, political violence is more likely.[294] In these situations, the growing peasant population tends to grow its crops on marginal land. Unable to generate enough food or income, peasants often rebel against local landlords, which can lead to political violence. In this example, it is important to keep in mind that population growth in itself did not cause the violence. Instead, it is population growth combined with a particular type of land distribution and economic structure that leads to violence.[295]

In urban areas, rapid population growth can lead to social and political instability if the economy is unable to create new jobs fast enough to absorb the growing working age population.[296] According to one estimate, some 45 million people will enter the jobs market in developing countries each year until 2015. The same study concludes that "this will place an enormous strain on economies that are already struggling to foster growth and keep populations productive".[297] Masses of unemployed young people are a breeding ground for the formation of extremist groups and violent behaviour. What has been referred to as a "youth bulge" – the presence of an exceptionally large number of 15 to 25 year old people in proportion to the rest of the population in urban areas – has been correlated with a rise in ethnic conflict.[298] If these young unemployed people are well-educated, the problem becomes even worse. According to Keely, "Not only do the young urbanites lack access to employment or political power, they have the time, intellectual resources, and organizational skills to create instability of various sorts and threaten prevailing structures".[299]

As is mentioned above, population growth occurs very unevenly across different cultures. One study predicts that by 2025, "industrial democracies may account for less than one-fourteenth of the total population of large countries".[300] This growing population imbalance may lead to new, culturally based divisions and tensions, as the world's largest cultural groups feel economically and/or politically disadvantaged vis-à-vis the, mostly Western, minority.[301]

In short, population growth does not automatically pose a threat to anyone's security. Rather, demographic factors can "increase the likelihood of problems or tend to exacerbate problems" in combination with particular economic and social circumstances.[302] Rapid population growth can put severe strains on resources and thus may precipitate resource-driven conflicts. Moreover, as Keely observes, mass migration, which can but does not have to be a result of rapid population growth, might ultimately be the most likely cause of demography-related security threats.[303]

(b) International Migration

Over 150 million people today live outside their country of birth.[304] Population growth, resource scarcity, lack of employment opportunities, civil wars, prospects for a better life in a wealthier country, and cheap and easy means of travel are all factors that have contributed to the growth in the number of migrants in recent decades. It becomes increasingly difficult for states to control who is entering their territory, which requires states to cooperate closely to improve border security. A case in point is the European Union's Schengen Agreement, which effectively creates a single border around the EU and provides for police cooperation and information sharing between EU member states.[305]

Mass migration can pose security threats to states that are already weakened or that maintain a delicate ethnic balance. Mass migration can occur for many different reasons. Most of these reasons are the consequences of some of the security threats discussed in this chapter. Mass migration can occur as a result of state failure or collapse; migrants may be fleeing intra-state wars or government persecution. Migrants may also leave their home country because they are no longer able to make a living due to widespread unemployment or shortages of arable land. Rapid population growth and environmental degradation may put strains on countries, which can lead some people to leave in anticipation of a better future in a different country.

Migration flows can cause security challenges for receiving countries. In developed countries such as those in Europe and North America, the settlement of a large number of immigrants from different cultural and religious backgrounds is causing social tensions. Europe especially has experienced a rise in right-wing parties, which can polarise domestic politics. The formation of violent groupings among immigrants who feel excluded and alienated from the rest of society is also a potential threat to social peace. However, putting artificial restrictions on immigration is often not feasible. Today, immigration quotas based on race and nationality are no longer in tune with international norms of racial equality and human rights. Moreover, it is sometimes not feasible for states to be selective about which immigrants to accept if they depend on foreign labour to fill job vacancies.[306] In the northern hemisphere, where birth rates have been declining rapidly and states are dealing with an aging population, countries increasingly rely on migrant workers to achieve economic growth.

Migrants can pose challenges to a state's national identity. National identity can be based on either a shared set of civic values or common ethnicity.[307] In either case, national identity provides the glue that holds members of a state together, helps to ensure mutual trust among citizens and, hence, promotes social cohesion. According to Fiona B. Adamson, states with a very diverse population due to the large number of migrants may lose a coherent sense of national identity and with it the ability to formulate "a coherent set of national interests".[308]

Some states, however, are resilient enough to adapt to their new, multicultural population and move to more "civil forms of nationalism".[309] Moreover, states can enhance their relative strength through good immigration policies. For one, migrant workers can benefit industrialised countries economically, by filling vacant job positions and contributing to the aging population's social security benefits.[310] Also, states that are able to make their job market attractive to highly skilled migrant workers are in a better position to maintain their technological edge. This can also have positive implications for a country's defence sector, which is becoming more and more high-tech. In addition, national intelligence services in many states can benefit from the foreign language expertise offered by some skilled migrants.[311]

In countries with a delicate ethnic balance, the influx of a large number of migrants with the same ethnic background as either the majority group or minority groups can pose serious political challenges. As Idean Salehyan and Kristian Skrede Gleditsch explain: "Majority groups in receiving areas may perceive a threat to their dominant status if refugees are similar to domestic minorities; and minority groups may feel that the influx of foreigners further dilutes their strength."[312] Migrants may also cause real or imagined strains on host countries' natural resources and employment situation – another reason why migrants can become a scapegoat for a country's problems, this time in the economic realm.

The largest challenges to national security, however, are posed by migrants from conflict zones. War refugees can pose challenges for various reasons. First, these refugees may bring weapons with them, which they may use to instigate cross-border attacks against their home government. Second, they may continue their violent struggle against ethnic rivals in their new host country.[313] Third, they may be traumatised by what they have lived through and consequently more easily use violence in their daily life.

Nevertheless, the influx of large numbers of migrants alone does not automatically shake the foundations of states. The stronger a state's institutions, the better its ability to regulate migration. Moreover, only in states where resources are already scarce, ethnic rivalries are already brewing, or social cohesion and government legitimacy are already weak will large numbers of migrants be able to plunge a state into a political crisis or worse. In short, mass migration hurts the weakest and poorest states in the world the most.

In turn, migration can hurt sending states as well. For instance, developing countries often lose their most highly skilled workers to other countries, which prevents these countries from building up their economies.[314] Yet ultimately, neither population growth nor migration per se pose direct security challenges to states. What matters, from a security perspective, are the circumstances under which these demographic developments occur.

3. The Information Revolution and National Security

The rapid development and spread of new ICT in the past two decades has left almost no aspect of human life untouched. The advancement of ICT has been nothing short of revolutionary. According to a 1996 report by the US-based Institute for National Strategic Studies (INSS), "What makes the information explosion so revolutionary is not that technology is advancing but the pace at which it improves...[N]ever before have societies been forced to adapt to a technology which for decades has been improving by an order of magnitude every three or four years".[315] Access to information is a prerequisite for economic growth in any country today.[316] As one author observes, "Mastery of information technology – whether exercised through commercial or military channels – is surpassing mastery of heavy industry as the primary source of national power."[317] The information revolution can further increase the gap between developing countries and the developed world, as poor people with little education are unable to enter the information-based economy.[318] As is discussed in section 5, an ever wider economic gap between states does not bode well for international stability.

Information technology can be employed to both undermine and further state security. Information technology can be used among states to coordinate security strategies and exchange crucial information. Similarly, it can be put to good use to coordinate peace support operations. It can also be used to spread awareness of potential security threats and to launch public campaigns in favour of outlawing particularly heinous kinds of weapons, such as landmines.[319] The information revolution is certainly transforming national defence requirements, which, in many ways, places states with a highly developed information technology sector at an advantage, as national militaries will increasingly have to invest in sophisticated information systems in order to keep up with potential enemies.

It should also be kept in mind that states are not powerless when it comes to regulating ICT. They can work on developing new technologies to track down terrorist groups more effectively and improve their surveillance capabilities.[320] As Geoffrey L. Herrera explains, states in principle have the legal authority and ability to regulate "the architecture of the infosphere".[321] However, putting the infosphere under government surveillance would run counter to the interests of private companies and violate democratic principles of free speech. Governments in open societies will therefore have to perform a delicate balancing act between the need to track down people bent on causing death and disruption and the need to protect civil liberties.

The new information technology, which has changed the way we work, communicate, trade, shop and access information, also has wide implications for the security sector. In particular, this section highlights potential ways of misusing or sabotaging global information networks to cause harm and discusses the role of the global media in international security politics.

(a) Cyberthreats and Information Warfare

Cyberthreats to computer networks constitute the most worrying misuse of information technology from a national security perspective. Cyberthreats involve a broad variety of actions that compromise or destroy the flow of information among computer networks. This can be done through the use of malicious software, such as by introducing computer viruses, but also by way of so-called denial-of-service attacks, which disrupt the flow of information.[322] In addition, cyber attacks can include the use of eavesdropping devices to gather information exchanged through computer networks.[323] Certainly, the latter can also be employed by states to further national security objectives by undermining the operations of terrorist or hostile states.

Due to the complexity of modern computer systems, and based on current experience, it appears that it will be virtually impossible to make modern computer systems immune from cyber attacks anytime in the foreseeable future.[324] According to one study, if the email virus infection rate continues to rise, we will reach a point at which the Internet could become unusable.[325]

Many cyber attacks, however, are financially motivated. Criminals or terrorist groups seek to enrich themselves through "banking fraud, credit card fraud, extortion, stock manipulation, scams, and theft of intellectual property".[326] As either an intended or unintended side effect, these types of attacks can, in the worst case, cause severe damage to national and international economies.

Some states have started to develop capabilities for offensive information warfare.[327] These government programmes develop the means and know-how to conduct effective computer network attacks to gather and/or disrupt strategic information exchanges within enemy countries. Other forms of information warfare that can be employed by states are "psychological operations and perception management".[328] "Well-developed computer-network-attack capability[ies]" might enable states to interrupt power and oil supply networks and "shut down transportation and communications systems".[329]

(b) Misusing the Internet to Spread Harmful Information

The Internet, as a global and easily accessible communication tool, has made it very easy to pass on information to people around the world within seconds. Moreover, powerful Internet search engines allow people to find a wealth of information on almost any topic in just a few mouse clicks. Despite all the benefits of the Internet, web-based information and communication tools can also be used by people for evil or illegal purposes. In the same way that e-mail allows family members and friends to stay in touch, e-mails can be used by criminal or terrorist organisations to organise their activities.

As has been thoroughly discussed in an earlier book, *The Emergence of Blogs as* a Fifth Estate *and Their Security Implications*, the emergence of blogs, and their ease of use to spread information on the Internet in real time, is one example of a new web-based communication tool that could potentially pose new dangers to the security of states.[330] For instance, blogs may become powerful vehicles for terrorist and criminal groups to spread information quickly and widely. As is noted in the book, "The unique structure of blogs ensures that even if one blog gets shut down or chooses to remove a posting, hundreds of others would have picked up the message by then, and stopping a particular posting from proliferating would become virtually impossible".[331] Blogs thus can "immortalise" information by spreading sensitive, false or defamatory information widely and in an uncontrolled way.[332] As the study concludes, "For governments, [the] possibility of losing all control over the information being traded within the country's borders may be perceived as a major threat to internal stability."[333]

Blogs may be used to make public but potentially sensitive information easily accessible to groups and individuals by reposting it on widely read blogs. Examples of such information that might be used by criminals or terrorists for illegal ends might be instructions on how to create explosive devices, "aerial and satellite images and maps of critical infrastructures" or the "names and assignments of government agents fighting crime and terrorism".[334] Furthermore, blogs can be used to explain this publicly available information to its readers and to add additional insights.

(c) The Global Media

The global media has a strong impact on security-related decision making. Global news networks such as the US-based Cable News Network (CNN) and the British Broadcasting Corporation (BBC) report news from the world's flash-points 24 hours a day, making the public and politicians around the world much better informed about violence and security threats originating from almost any corner of the world. Global media reporting on instances of massive human rights violations, for example, increases the popular pressure on politicians to stop the violence.[335] Security officials, particularly in the developed world, can no longer ignore issues that may not be priorities on their own security agenda, but are prominently reported by the global media.

The global media can also have an important impact on power-political configurations. Global news today is dominated by the Western, especially the US, media. As Diana Owen explains, this creates a serious imbalance as to whose interests and views regarding world politics are being spread: "As global media presence translates into global political power, nations with superior communications technology have a greater hold over the flow of information and the construction of international images".[336]

The exclusion of non-Western voices from global news may breed growing resentment among peoples whose views are either not represented or only represented through Western eyes.[337] Market forces are imposing further constraints on media corporations. To cut operational costs and raise profits, many international media organisations have cut the number of international correspondents and started to rely on press agencies for information, which is making their reports increasingly uniform.[338]

In today's competitive media market, Owen explains, the media, eager to report on issues without verifying the truthfulness of their reports and without considering the political and humanitarian consequences that their reports may have, can compromise security: "the possibility for information to be disseminated in ways that compromise national security interests is intensified as news organizations focus on the bottom line and lack the foresight and experience to anticipate the consequences of their actions".[339] For Owen, a case in point is CNN's footage of the bodies of US soldiers being dragged through the streets of Mogadishu in October 1993, which, according to some accounts, increased public pressure and influenced President Clinton's decision to withdraw US troops from Somalia.[340]

Moreover, the media can affect public support for a particular policy by the way it covers the event. Public officials tasked with enhancing national security thus become constrained in their actions by the way the media reports on the policy. As Owen explains, "The public perceptions of and reactions to events are an important component of security affairs, and they are shaped largely by media coverage".[341] The media both selects the issues it wants to broadcast, and thus which world events the public will be paying attention to, and at the same time shapes public perceptions of world events.[342]

The term "CNN effect" is sometimes used to describe the global media's ability to influence US foreign policy making. According to Owen, "The 'CNN effect' implies a loss of policymaking control on the part of decision makers because of the power and immediacy of press reports. Driven by American media values, this situation promotes a foreign policy of media-specific crisis management."[343] The ability of a government to influence media reports about its country's actions will have a huge effect on the country's international prestige and power.

Moreover, the proliferation of media outlets and Internet news sources poses a challenge to public officials trying to identify security threats by sifting through floods of often contradictory information. Determining the accuracy and completeness of conflicting news reports is often a daunting task. Moreover, news outlets – and even individual bloggers – can spread information instantaneously and globally. In other words, power becomes increasingly vested in the individuals and institutions that manage and spread information.[344]

States will have more and more difficulty insulating their population from information originating from outside their borders, which will have various consequences for national security. For instance, the widespread availability of satellite television in the developing world has led to a greater awareness of the large economic gap between rich and poor countries. Knowledge about the quality of life in the developed world can lead to rising expectations among the populations of developing countries. This may lead people to rebel against their own government if they feel that their government's economic development programme is not progressing fast enough. This, in turn, can cause severe political instability, which is unlikely to help the cause of speeding up national economic development. However, growing popular resentment can be turned not just against the national government, but also against wealthier countries and the "leaders" of the globalisation process – especially the United States. The perception among people in the developing world that they are being left behind and unable to reap the fruits of economic globalisation might make them vulnerable to extremist, anti-globalisation and anti-Western ideologies. Another possible consequence might be growing legal and illegal migration to wealthy countries,[345] which, as is discussed above, can cause social problems in receiving states.

4. Transcivilizational Interactions

Economic globalisation and increased social mobility have multiplied interactions between members of different cultures and civilizations. In a globalising world, the clash between different national and multicultural values is inevitable. Different cultural communities have to deal with questions of identity and change, and with what sets them apart from others versus how to adapt to new cultural influences and technological innovations. Similarly, states are increasingly confronted with questions of national identity.

There are many collective entities in the world that do not correspond to state borders. These entities may either make up a group within a state or span state borders. These communities are formed by individuals who identify with each other based, for example, on a shared ethnicity, language or religion, or a common history. The collective identity of such cultural communities can be threatened by "migration, competition with a neighbouring or dominant culture, and de-population".[346] Due to increased global interconnectedness and an intensification of migratory movements, contacts and interactions between different cultural communities are intensified. Moreover, improved information and communication technology allows people to make instant connections with each other. This can have both positive and negative consequences. On the one hand, it can lead to increased open-mindedness and tolerance among cultural communities willing to engage in a fruitful exchange of ideas and knowledge with other communities. On the other hand, if cultural communities feel that their identity is under threat, they may turn to xenophobia and exclusionary tendencies to drive a wedge between themselves and the "other". If hostilities between diverse cultural entities occur within a state that has failed to promote a common national identity among those groups, or that visibly discriminates against certain cultural groups in favour of others, state stability can become seriously undermined.

As the global economy is strongly dominated by Western, and especially US, values and culture, it is non-Western cultural communities that have to make the largest cultural adaptations as they integrate into the global economy. Social entities that are undergoing particularly rapid technological and cultural changes as a result of globalisation and rapid economic development tend to be the most prone to develop reactionary and defensive tendencies.[347] Also, such rapid changes may create tensions within cultures between those willing to embrace Western ideas and technologies and those rejecting them.

The notion that not just cultural, but also civilizational entities can be a source of insecurity has been elaborated by political scientist Samuel P. Huntington. Huntington's well-known "clash of civilizations" thesis argues that the wars of the future will no longer be fought between states or ideological "camps" but between the world's major civilizations. Huntington defines civilization as "a cultural entity" which constitutes "the highest cultural grouping of people and the broadest level of cultural identity people have short of that which distinguishes humans from other species".[348] The major civilizational groups he identifies "include Western, Confucian, Japanese, Islamic, Hindu, Slavic-Orthodox, Latin American and possibly African civilization".[349] Due to globalisation, Huntington explains, peoples of different civilizations will come to interact with each other more closely, which will enhance "civilization consciousness and awareness of differences between civilizations and commonalities within civilizations".[350] In terms of power relationships, the West is by far the most powerful civilizational group – it has both military and economic superiority over the rest of the world. Western powers dominate the UN Security Council and international economic institutions, such as the International Monetary Fund (IMF). Due to this imbalance, Huntington posits, "the paramount axis of world politics will be the relations between 'the West and the Rest.'"[351]

Huntington's thesis and predictions for the future, however, have triggered a lot of scholarly debate. Many scholars have pointed out flaws in Huntington's line of reasoning. Niall Ferguson, for example, makes the observation that the vast majority of wars in the post-Cold War era have been intra-state wars fought between ethnic groups that were part of the same "civilization".[352] Ferguson expects this trend to continue, stating that "multiple local wars," rather than "a global collision of value-systems" will dominate the future landscape, and that these ethnic conflicts ultimately weaken the world's different civilizational blocs.[353] Indeed, globalisation might actually help to mitigate cultural clashes by facilitating the creation of transnational networks and spreading common global norms and values.

Jonathan Kirshner predicts that the global market, which becomes more and more pervasive in the lives of people in non-Western societies, will provoke backlashes. According to Kirshner, the "values of secular capitalism" that globalisation promotes include "universalism, materialism, and consumerism"; yet at the same time, "many alternate value systems, including national, cultural, and social movements, will offer resistance".[354] Organised religion, he believes, will become an important unifying force for people seeking an alternative to the values promoted through marketisation.[355] Religious movements will reflect the new global culture in the sense that they are likely to organise transnationally. Hence, writes Kirshner, these groups become both "an expression of globalization and a reaction to it".[356]

In sum, globalisation has clearly intensified transcultural and transcivilizational interactions. Individuals, cultural communities and states have to adapt to this new fact of life. Isolation is not a viable option, and peaceful coexistence alone no longer a sufficient one in the 21st century. As Hans Koechler argues: "The self-comprehension of a civilization and the appreciation of its values have to be embedded in an inter-civilizational framework of mutual exchange. Civilizations that aspire to be present in the global framework today have to accept the fact of interdependence."[357] As is suggested in an earlier work, a synergy between the world's different cultures and civilizations needs to be created.[358] Such a synergy would constitute a powerful force to promote international understanding, peace and security.

5. Growing Economic Cleavages and Energy Security

Economic globalisation is having an effect on geopolitical configurations – the extent of this effect, however, is not yet clear. Some have argued that economic power is becoming of greater geopolitical importance than traditional military capabilities, and that economic competition is increasingly replacing military competition between the great powers in the 21st century.[359] The global economy may help some states to become more powerful – especially states with a vibrant economy that can benefit from trade liberalisation.

A parallel development is that national governments are slowly losing control of their national economies. Some states try to counteract economic integration by pursuing protectionist policies to protect key economic sectors from being crowded out by foreign competitors. Such attempts, however, might just be a symptom of the fact that the increased mobility of global capital means that states are no longer in a position to effectively regulate and control economic transactions.[360]

At the same time, the global economy takes away power from states because governments no longer have the choice to pursue alternative economic policies if they want to continue to compete in the global market, and states have less power to successfully counteract undesirable trends in their national economies. In fact, multinational and transnational corporations today could be considered actors on their own in international relations due to their increasingly strong influence on national governments.[361] States' dependence on attracting and keeping MNCs in their country sometimes induces states to reduce regulation and protection for employees, such as health and safety standards.

(a) Global Poverty and the Gap Between Rich and Poor

The global economy has both winners and losers. Many analysts fear that the economic gap between rich and poor states will continue to widen. The information revolution and ideas-based value production plays a role as it leaves those countries unable to keep up with new technological developments further and further behind.[362]

Rising global inequality has many strategic implications for the developed world. For instance, it can trigger new causes for violence and aggression. For one, some states may try to distract from domestic economic discontent and engage in adventurism abroad, pursuing regional military hegemony in an attempt to make up for their economic inferiority.[363] Other poverty-stricken states may try to acquire WMD, especially nuclear weapons, to enhance their bargaining power vis-à-vis stronger states.[364]

Rising global inequality poses long-term risks to the global economic system. This is especially true with regard to the external debt owed by developing countries, which in 2001 amounted to about USD2.3 trillion.[365] Vincent Ferraro explains that writing off these debts entirely would inflict "irreparable damage to the future integrity of the international financial system".[366] Moreover, he goes on, "outright defaults on these loans would perhaps fatally undermine confidence in global capital markets and critically weaken specific banks with substantial outstanding loans".[367] Ferraro thus concludes that the fates of wealthy and poor states today are interlinked, because it is clearly in the interests of rich states that poor states reach a certain degree of economic development that will allow them to repay at least some of their debts.[368] Similarly, the economic success of developing countries will benefit wealthy states due to the higher returns from trade and investments.[369]

Economic collapse or rapid economic decline are the main causes of state failure, with all its negative security implications discussed above. As Jeffrey Sachs reminds us, historical examples of a severe economic crisis leading to war and turmoil abound; for instance, both the rise of the Bolsheviks and the rise of Hitler occurred during times of economic crisis.[370] At the same time, democracies, which purportedly do not go to war against each other, tend to be more stable if citizens enjoy an adequate standard of living. The global economy can only flourish in a stable international environment where there are few disruptions to international commerce and global production cycles. Narrowing the growing chasm between rich and poor states is in the long-term economic and security interests of every state.

(b) Resource Distribution

Securing national energy supplies remains a key issue in 21st century geopolitics. Oil is the lifeline of the global economy, and any disruption to oil supply will have dramatic economic consequences. Oil is the single largest source of the world's primary energy, and it will continue to be so in the foreseeable future. With continued economic growth and development, especially in the developing world, demand for this precious resource is unlikely to diminish. On the contrary, global demand for oil is expected to increase by over 42 percent in the next two decades.[371]

Oil is a finite resource. When exactly regular crude oil reaches its half-life, that is, the point at which global oil production is at its absolute maximum, also referred to the as global peak oil, is disputed among analysts. Some say that that the peak of global oil production will be reached in a couple of decades, while others argue that this is happening right now.[372] A fact, however, is that no abundant new sources of oil have been explored in recent years. According to the *Energy Bulletin*, "today only one new barrel of oil is being discovered for every four that are extracted and used."[373]

What is more, most of the world's known oil reserves are concentrated in a very small area of the world – the Middle East has about 60 percent of global oil reserves,[374] and 90 percent of Middle Eastern oil is located in only five countries: Saudi Arabia, Iraq, Iran, Kuwait and the United Arab Emirates (UAE).[375] Meanwhile, oil reserves in the northern hemisphere have already reached their peak. The United States, for example, formerly the world's largest oil producer, hit its all-time high in 1971.[376]

Tom W. O'Donnell argues that the uneven geographic distribution of resources can have geopolitical consequences: "geographic concentration of a natural resource raises the possibility of a single state or of a small number of states (acting in concert) exerting predominant influence (that is hegemony) in mediating global access to that resource".[377] Moreover, some of the key energy pipelines and key sea lanes for oil shipments run through disputed territories. Transportation routes in the South and East China Seas are jeopardised due to disputed territorial claims.[378] As one author cautions, energy pipelines and transmission grids may be sabotaged by "terrorists, hackers [and] disaffected local groups".[379]

There are also environmental security aspects related to the growth in fossil fuel consumption. Producing fewer greenhouse gases and reducing pollution caused by the burning of fossil fuels to stave off global warming will be in the long-term national security interests of every state, as is discussed further below.

6. Transnational Organised Crime

Transnational organised crime, sometimes dubbed the "dark underside of the global economy", can pose serious challenges to the national security of states.[380] These global criminal networks may be engaged in human smuggling or trafficking or illicit trade in drugs and arms. They can undermine state authority "by corrupting government institutions; endanger a state's financial and economic stability; and violate legal rules, property rights, and human rights".[381]

In cases where criminal networks succeed in infiltrating governments or bribe public officials and judges, a state's autonomy becomes seriously compromised. Even if criminal networks "only" seem to cause internal law-enforcement problems, their existence can pose security threats across borders. If their activities undermine a country's political, economic and social infrastructure, other states will eventually be affected.[382] Organised crime can contribute strongly to state instability and state weakness, with all the transnational threats associated with it.

In states that possess WMD, the existence of powerful organised criminal groups can heighten the danger of these groups coming into possession of lethal weapons, which they might in turn sell to terrorist groups.[383]

The production and international distribution of illegal narcotics by organised criminal groups has many negative social and economic consequences for states. In the United States, illegal drug consumption costs the federal government over USD100 billion a year.[384] Widespread drug addiction weakens a country's social fabric, as it often contributes to a surge in criminal activity and prostitution, the spread of disease, especially HIV/AIDS, and a decline in productive capacity. The existence of a widespread drug economy reduces a country's potential for regular economic growth. Even worse, the drug trade can criminalise a country's peace economy.[385]

Furthermore, drugs can fuel violent internal conflicts. The proceeds from the sale of illegal narcotics have helped various rebel and terrorist groups around the world to fund their operations. Violent conflicts over the control of drug cultivation and sales may also precipitate internal conflicts within countries.[386]

According to UN estimates, transnational organised crime generates USD1–1.5 trillion per year.[387] National economies in small developing countries in particular can be outpaced by criminal activities. The proceeds from organised crime do not usually create regular jobs, and it may only divert capable workers from regular jobs.[388] Organised crime thus severely hampers economic development in poor states.

Not only from a national security standpoint, but also from a purely humanitarian perspective, the increase in human smuggling and trafficking incidences since the end of the Cold War is a worrying development. Human smuggling refers to the transport of illegal immigrants to a (usually wealthier) country of their choice in exchange for money. Human trafficking involves the employment of measures of deception or raw force to recruit mostly women and children for the purpose of exploiting them as slave labourers or prostitutes.[389] The number of trafficking victims is estimated to be about 200 million.[390] It is thought to be the fastest growing international criminal activity today.[391] The expansion of human trafficking and forced labour primarily causes socio-economic problems for states, as it depresses wages and deprives child victims of an education. Equally worrying, however, is the ease with which humans with illegal intentions are able to cross national borders – which suggests that if millions of human beings are being trafficked or smuggled across borders, other people with even more dangerous intentions, such as terrorists, may also be.

7. Non-state Actors, Terrorism and Asymmetrical Warfare

The emergence of resourceful non-state actors, including terrorist networks and violent groups formed around religious extremism or anti-globalisation, poses new threats to national security. Unlike military threats emanating from other states, non-state actors can hardly be defeated by regular national armies and conventional military tactics.

(a) Asymmetrical Warfare

Asymmetrical warfare refers to a form of combat where "one side fights conventionally while the other side organises itself differently…and rejects the conventions or laws of warfare propounded by the conventional side".[392] It is usually the weaker party that uses unconventional means as a way of countering the opponent's technological or numerical superiority.[393]

Analyst Martin van Creveld has argued that traditional wars between state armies are no longer common, and that asymmetrical wars are the wars of the future. He predicts that "In the future, wars will not be waged by armies but by groups whom we today call terrorists, guerrillas, bandits and robbers.…Their organizations are likely to be constructed on charismatic lines rather than institutional ones, and to be motivated less by 'professionalism' than by fanatical, ideologically based loyalties."[394] In this form of warfare, there are no definable fronts. Fighting is dispersed, and the distinction between combatants and civilians will become meaningless in terms of targeting.[395] Moreover, as Snow explains, "[t]he goal will not be traditional military defeat, but instead the internal political collapse of the opponent and its will to continue."

(b) Terrorism

Terrorism is one form of asymmetrical warfare and constitutes a type of violence that is unlikely to go away anytime soon. Terrorism may be defined as the deliberate targeting of civilians in order to spread fear. It is usually an indirect way of pressuring a government to comply with the demands of a terrorist group.

The difficulty with terrorism for national security officials is that it can never be entirely defeated. Terrorism describes a tactic, a set of means by which a technologically and numerically weaker group seeks to put pressure on a much stronger enemy to achieve its objectives. The tactic may be as old as human civilization. Snow thus suggests differentiating between the idea of terrorism – which can be publicly repudiated using moral arguments – and individual terrorist groups, whose members can be targeted and subdued.[396] Although states may succeed at improving their counterterrorism efforts and at devising increasingly efficient tactics to hunt down individual terrorists, terrorism as an abstract and potential threat to national security will always remain. Because our relative sense of security is strongly influenced by subjective perceptions and psychological factors, whether real or imagined, the threat of terrorism is likely to continue to loom large on the national security agendas of states.

Currently, most terrorist activity occurs in the Middle East and North Africa; however, places like Central and South Asia, the Balkans and Transcaucasia have recently gained in significance in this regard.[397] Similarly, immigrant communities in Western Europe, where many immigrants are poorly integrated into society, feel disoriented and uprooted, and often lack good job prospects, may continue to be breeding grounds for terrorist activity in Europe.

Terrorist have also become more effective due to advances in ICT, such as cellular phones and the Internet. This allows terrorist groups to cooperate with each other, recruit members, and plan more sophisticated and coordinated attacks. The Internet also helps terrorists to spread and share their extremist ideologies better and faster. Because "true extremists tend to be in short supply", the Internet can be helpful for finding recruits.[398]

According to one expert, terrorist groups today have the potential to create serious setbacks to the globalisation process.[399] He contends that what most international terrorist groups have in common is their opposition to globalisation.[400] Because there will continue to be large gaps between those benefiting from globalisation and those who feel left behind, he believes that the motivation that leads people to join or support terrorist groups will not diminish anytime soon:[401] "At times of dramatic international change, human beings (especially those not benefiting from the change, or not benefiting as much or as rapidly from the change) grasp for alternative means to control and understand their environments".[402]

8. Proliferation

What used to worry national security officials about weapons proliferation during the Cold War was mainly the arms race between the major powers – so-called vertical proliferation.[403] Since the mid-1980s, but especially since the early 1990s, security experts have started to become seriously concerned about the acquisition of lethal weapons by less developed and less stable states – so-called horizontal proliferation.[404] Rogue states have become a primary focus of concern in counterproliferation, as have non-state groups, including terrorists, bent on acquiring WMD capability to launch mass-casualty attacks.[405]

Horizontal weapons proliferation is a security issue that is inextricably linked to economic globalisation.[406] The increase in international trade and the decrease in trade barriers make it almost impossible for states to fully control what goes in and out of the country and, with regard to sensitive technology, what the final destination of the product in question is. Moreover, growing interconnectedness through international travel and global communication has helped to make sensitive know-how regarding weapons technology more widely available.[407] In addition, modern communication tools, including the Internet and encryption countermeasures, allow weapons proliferation networks to organise across borders.[408]

The economic and social freedoms that individuals and corporations have come to enjoy as a result of economic globalisation thus come with a price. The interests of global commerce in the further liberalisation of trade and the security interests of states in controlling the dissemination of sensitive technology and know-how are to a certain extent irreconcilable.[409] Hence, weapons proliferation is a security problem that will continue to plague states in the decades to come.

(a) WMD

The term WMD generally refers to nuclear, chemical, biological and radiological weapons. An important distinguishing feature between WMD and conventional weapons is that employing them makes it virtually impossible to discriminate between combatants and non-combatants. WMD are particularly heinous as they cause unacceptable deaths among civilians.

Today, several states, especially in the developing world, are engaged in an ambitious pursuit of WMD. These states perceive the possession of WMD as a way of enhancing their bargaining power and prestige vis-à-vis other states, as well as an effective deterrent. Ballistic missiles are usually the delivery system of choice among these states. Due to the development of sophisticated technologies in this field, including navigational aids, such as global positioning systems, and air-breathing carriers, such as cruise missiles, delivery systems have become very effective and relatively inexpensive.[410]

Unfortunately, preventing states from acquiring these technologies will prove to be an almost impossible undertaking. First, some potential proliferators have been able to set up their own domestic missile technology and WMD programmes and are thus becoming less dependent on outside help.[411] Second, some of the technology and materials used for WMD missile development are readily available on the global market as they are also used for peaceful non-military purposes.[412] Third, globalisation makes it increasingly easy to obtain WMD materiel on the black market.[413] The break-up of the Soviet Union has contributed to the problem. Some of the nuclear material stockpiles are no longer as tightly guarded as they were during Soviet times, which increases the possibility of this material falling into the hands of organised criminal networks that would then sell it to states or even terrorist groups.

The acquisition of the ultimate WMD, a nuclear capability, by states that are unstable or have an aggressive posture is a growing security concern. At the same time, recent policies by some of the established nuclear powers have raised fears that the taboo among civilised countries on the use of nuclear weapons is withering away in the moral consciousness of some political and military leaders. For instance, US plans to develop smaller tactical nuclear weapons such as the so-called bunker busters are sometimes interpreted as an attempt to make nuclear weapons more "usable". Moreover, the fact that two new nuclear weapon states, India and Pakistan, are still engaged in a military conflict over Kashmir has heightened concerns that nuclear weapons might one day be used.[414]

Chemical and biological weapons are especially popular among smaller and less resourceful states eager to develop a WMD capability. They are less expensive than nuclear weapons, and most of the technologies and materials needed to produce them can be obtained legally on the international market. Furthermore, chemical and biological weapon programmes can be developed in secret, away from the eyes of international inspectors.[415] Often, the technology with which these weapons are produced is dual use: civilian plants can easily be turned into production facilities for chemical and biological weapons.[416]

Biological and chemical weapons are outlawed by widely accepted international treaties. The Chemical Weapons Convention, in force since 1997, and the Biological Weapons Convention, in force since 1975, prohibit the production and possession of these types of weapons.[417] The Chemical Weapons Convention includes verification measures, whereas the Biological Weapons Convention does not. Some signatories to the Biological Weapons Convention are nonetheless suspected of maintaining biological weapon programmes.[418] What is more, not all states are party to the conventions and others are slow to destroy their existing stockpiles.

Among the civilised world, the use of chemical and biological weapons is more or less taboo and considered inherently immoral. However, these moral constraints will not deter terrorists or rogue states from using them. As one study puts it, "If terrorist groups seek to inflict psychological wounds on their targets, norm-breaking actions may be increasingly favored".[419] The increased availability of WMD is a worrying development, and security experts in the 21st century will have to continue to grapple with the question of how their spread can be effectively contained.

(b) Small Arms

Perhaps not as headline grabbing as WMD proliferation, but in many ways equally worrying in security terms, is the proliferation of conventional weapons, including small arms. As one author notes, the motivations for arms transfers have clearly changed since the end of the Cold War. During the Cold War, the supply of arms to other states was largely politically driven, with the United States and the Soviet Union being the dominant arms suppliers at the time.[420] Today, arms are sold mostly for economic gain.

The dissolution of the Soviet Union and the ensuing breakdown in law and order both in Russia and the former Soviet republics led to the dissemination of large amounts of small arms from former Soviet military and police forces, which today are frequently sold on the black market.[421] Other sources of weapons are former conflict zones, where small arms, still widespread but no longer in use, are sold off and recycled in other conflicts.[422]

Illegal small arms trafficking can be both a result of and a precipitating factor in state weakness and failure. Arms sold on the black market often supply rebel groups in areas torn by internal conflicts such as the former Yugoslavia, Afghanistan and many African states. According to the United Nations, illegally sold small arms constituted "a significant element in 46 of 49 major conflicts in the 1990s" and cause about 500,000 deaths per year.[423] As yet, there is no satisfactory mechanism in place to control the flow of small arms. Apart from the practical difficulties of controlling the illegal flow of small arms, there is also a broad lack of political will among exporting states to reduce the quantity of legal arms sales.

9. The Privatisation of Security

The 21st century might be seeing a "rebirth" of mercenary armies, as private security companies (PSCs) are currently on the rise. PSCs provide services to armed forces, such as technical support, and sometimes even contribute troops. In post-war Iraq, for instance, PSCs assist US forces in conducting policing jobs.[424] According to one study, "The ratio of US troops to PSC personnel in the 2003 Iraq war has been estimated at 1:10, and since the formal ending of the war in May 2003 the number of contractors has increased".[425] Furthermore, MNCs increasingly hire private security firms for their protection. Cases in point are international oil companies hiring private protection forces to safeguard their installations in weak or unstable states.

In the short term, the increased use of PSCs may be financially advantageous for governments. For one, the ability to hire private security companies on demand allows governments to cut back on public forces, which have to be paid even when they are not needed. For another, encouraging organisations and companies in the private sector to organise and pay for their own protection also lightens the burden on state resources. In the longer term, however, extensive reliance on PSCs as an alternative to the public security apparatus can seriously undermine the authority of the state, which may lead to instability in states that are already weak.[426]

Private security forces are outside the control of states, and it is difficult to hold states accountable for actions committed by private security companies. Nor are states in control of the military training of PSC employees; for instance, they cannot be sure whether employees of the companies they are hiring have received adequate instruction in the laws of warfare, including the Geneva Conventions. Driven by the profit motive, PSCs may be tempted to circumvent legal or moral barriers to get their job done efficiently and at the lowest cost possible.

Furthermore, the stakes for going to war might become lower for elected leaders, as there is no need to mobilise troops and sacrifice the lives of drafted citizens. In democracies, this might also mean that citizens have less control over foreign policy. Governments might also be more likely to engage in adventurous policies when they can pursue them by hiring private companies.[427] Moreover, states that have shortages in their armed forces might be tempted to hire PSCs rather than build coalitions with other states and thus have a freer hand in conducting military campaigns.[428]

In short, the availability of PSCs loosens some of the constraints on states when going to war. At the same time, PSCs, unlike national armies, may perceive fewer constraints while fighting wars. International laws of warfare, including both *ius ad bellum* and *ius in bello*, will be affected by these new developments. The world of private security firms is still a highly unregulated market, and states will need to come up with ways to regulate the use and employment of PSCs.

10. Health, Diseases and Biosecurity

The spread of infectious diseases is not a new threat, but globalisation has increased the speed with which diseases are transmitted, as well as broadened their reach. Due to the pace and frequency of global travel, diseases can quickly spread across continents and are thus hard to contain. A virus carried by a traveller can move to another continent before the symptoms of the disease have broken out in the infected person.[429]

The most prominent infectious diseases in the past few years have been severe acute respiratory syndrome (SARS), avian influenza H5N1, West Nile virus and, of course, HIV/AIDS.[430] Other infectious diseases that have been around for a long time, but continue to threaten humans, such as tuberculosis, and livestock, such as bovine spongiform encephalopathy (popularly known as "mad cow disease") and foot-and-mouth disease, also need to be taken seriously.[431] On average, about one new infectious disease emerges every year.[432] According to a RAND study, "Approximately three-fourths of infectious diseases that have emerged and reemerged in recent decades are zoonoses, i.e., diseases transmitted to humans from animals".[433] Moreover, zoononic diseases can be transmitted by agricultural trade, which is particularly worrying because many national economies are heavily dependent on agricultural exports.[434] Rapid urbanisation, especially in the developing world, poses increased risks for disease transmission due to "poor sanitation, crowding, and sharing resources such as food and water".[435]

Infectious diseases can be a serious security issue. Currently, a quarter of all deaths in the world are caused by infectious diseases.[436] Leading among them are HIV/AIDS, tuberculosis, malaria, pneumonia and diarrhoeal diseases.[437] Developing countries are thereby hit especially hard. Public officials in many countries, including the United States, have braced themselves for the real possibility of an avian influenza epidemic, which would cause large numbers of casualties and enormous disruption to national economies. Furthermore, the isolation of countries affected by a pandemic would prevent the movement of goods and people across borders and thus lead to economic losses for affected countries and their trading partners. Indeed, economic losses due to disease can be devastating. One study estimates that Africa's gross domestic product (GDP) would be "nearly one-third higher if malaria alone had been eliminated several decades ago".[438] This estimate includes both indirect costs, such as loss of productivity and commerce, and direct economic costs, including medical expenses.[439] In Russia, HIV/AIDS and tuberculosis together claim one percent of the country's GDP each year – money that could be spent on other urgently needed government projects.[440] A government's inability to adequately contain infectious diseases can also de-legitimise governments in the eyes of their people, which in turn can lead to state instability.

Infectious diseases, such as HIV/AIDS in Africa, cause shortages in human capital and thus hamper economic development. In particular, about half of new HIV/AIDS infections in Africa occur among 15–24 year-olds – usually the most productive segment of society.[441] Furthermore, the disease deprives the country of a "core group of parents, social leaders, and key members of society, such as teachers and soldiers".[442] Because HIV/AIDS infection rates in Africa are particularly high among members of national armies, the disease may indirectly compromise the ability of some countries to effectively protect their borders.[443] Moreover, infectious diseases can cause severe social disruption, for example through "the loss of key social positions due to illness or death," or "discrimination against groups affected by a disease".[444]

Even if a country's population is not directly affected by a pandemic, the regional spread of a pandemic anywhere in the world is worrying nonetheless because infectious diseases can have serious security implications that can reverberate across the world. States hit by a pandemic can be severely destabilised. This is especially true for weak and poor states, which often lack the necessary health service infrastructures to contain the disease and treat infected people. The US State Department has gone so far as to consider disease as a potential war trigger.[445] A further concern regarding diseases originating in developing states is that some of these states lack the infrastructure and capacity to detect these new diseases early enough and thus fail to prevent the disease from spreading uncontrollably.[446]

11. Environmental Security

Concerns about the environment have traditionally been dealt with in the context of development and conservation. Today, its relevance to national and international security and stability is increasingly being acknowledged. Environmental destruction and resource scarcity can be a contributing cause for large refugee movements and increased tensions within and between states. Floods or a rise in sea levels may make portions of a state's territory uninhabitable or entirely disappear. The well-being of individuals is put in jeopardy as a result of air pollution, a lack of drinking water, or the erosion of arable land.[447] At best, environmental destruction can impede the progress of human civilization. At worst, it can jeopardise human existence on Earth. Environmental security implies that the natural environment needs to be protected as it constitutes the basis and prerequisite of human life and ultimately enables all human activities.[448]

Although humans have had an altering effect on the environment since the dawn of human existence, the post-World War II era, which saw massive population growth and a rapid increase in economic activity, has sped up this process enormously.[449] Any human civilization whose consumption of natural resources (including clean air, water, fertile soil, etc.) outstrips the environment's ability to renew itself is in the long-term unsustainable. Environmental security thus includes challenges ranging from climate change and water and air pollution to the depletion of non-renewable natural resources. The consequences of these environmental challenges may include an increased frequency of droughts, floods, land erosion and tornadoes; economic stagnation or severe destabilisation; and possibly an increase in human conflicts.

(a) Climate Change

Global warming refers to an overall increase in global temperatures as a result of greenhouse gas emissions coming mostly from the burning of fossil fuels. Even small increases – estimates range from between 1.8–4.0 degrees Celsius in global average surface temperatures by the year 2100[450] – will have devastating effects on our ecosystem. Different regions of the world will be affected by environmental changes and disasters differently and to different degrees, but the security implications are manifold. A 2007 UN Intergovernmental Panel on Climate Change (IPCC) report predicts consequences that mostly involve an increase in flooding and droughts.[451] For Africa, the IPCC predicts serious water shortages, which are expected to compromise agricultural production and thus food supply on the continent.[452] Growing resource and food scarcity due to global warming are likely to increase the number of refugees and internally displaced persons on a continent that already carries the burden of being the home of 30 percent of the world's refugees. Such developments are expected to further weaken governments and precipitate economic collapse.[453]

Similarly, the IPCC panel notes that in Central, South, East and Southeast Asia, shortages in freshwater availability due to receding glaciers combined with "population growth and increasing demand arising from higher standards of living, could aversely affect more than a billion people by the 2050s".[454]

At the same time, countries with large coastal plain and river areas, as well as small island states, will lose part of their territory due to the rise in sea levels. Considering that almost 40 percent of Asia's population lives within 45 miles of the coast, the potential rise in sea levels is of particular concern for this continent.[455] Bangladesh and parts of India are expected to be hit particularly hard, as well as China, where "the combination of sea-level rise and storm surges could create 50 million environmental refugees".[456] Flooding will also increase exposure to waterborne diseases, such as diarrhoeal disease and malaria.[457]

(b) Environmental Degradation and Resource Depletion
Shortages of basic natural resources – created either as a result of pollution, global warming or overconsumption – are expected to plague an increasing number of countries and regions in the years to come. For example, it is estimated that "Some 65 percent of the world's croplands are degraded and the percentage continues to grow".[458] Forests and fish stocks are being depleted at an alarming rate. Moreover, over one billion people today suffer from a shortage of safe drinking water.[459]

Shortages of vital resources have the potential to become hard power security issues. The lack of vital resources or arable land could lead to mass migration away from affected areas into more fertile regions, cities or other countries. The influx of large numbers of "environmental refugees" can cause pressure on land and might even lead to outbreaks of violence. Resource scarcity can also lead to widespread poverty and growing ethnic tensions. According to one author, "environmental change produces social change, leading to the fragmentation of states or, conversely, to a more authoritarian 'hardening' of the state."[460]

The depletion of water resources is a growing concern in many parts of the world. Today, between 30 and 40 states in southwest Asia and North Africa face serious water shortages. At the same time, these countries have very high population growth rates, so water supply in these countries is expected to become even more constrained.[461]

Although states are unevenly affected by environmental threats, the well-being of the natural habitat is in the long-term national security interest of every nation. Environmental changes in the 21st century are highly likely to cause security problems. First, environmental pollution and the effects of global warming know no borders, and the emission of greenhouse gases or other forms of environmental pollution in one state thus becomes a concern for everybody.[462]

Second, resource depletion and environmental pollution have the potential to lead indirectly to violent conflict either within states or between states.[463] However, the relationship between resource scarcity and violent conflict is unclear and remains subject to debate among academics and security experts. Some experts maintain that so-called resource wars will increasingly dominate the international landscape. To support their case, these experts point to the "increasing importance of economic concerns; increasing demand for basic commodities; instability in regions endowed with reserves of commodities; festering disputes over ownership and control of supplies; and impending shortages of basic, non-renewable commodities".[464]

However, scholars such as J.R. McNeill argue that conflicts are unlikely to be caused by resource scarcity alone. He takes water scarcity as a case in point. McNeill mentions a number of cases where possible friction over water might arise: "Ethiopia and Sudan could make very good use of the Nile water that makes Egypt viable…[while] Turkey…could find uses for the waters of the Tigris and Euphrates, the lifeblood of Syria and Iraq".[465] Yet, as McNeill points out, these possible frictions are unlikely to lead automatically to war. Instead, disputes over resources, such as water, could be one precipitating factor for armed hostilities between states that are already on bad terms with each other.[466] McNeill predicts that the Indus and Jordan rivers are the most likely waterways over which conflicts could break out, "as frictions are [already] great for other reasons".[467]

In sum, even states for which environmental security does not top the list of security concerns will have to start paying attention to the issue. As one author puts it, considering that many resource reserves and "ecological buffers", including "forests, unexploited fisheries, [and] unpolluted fresh water," are being depleted, "there is less slack in the human environment system now".[468]

As this chapter makes clear, many of the non-traditional threats to national security discussed above are interlinked. Resource scarcity has an effect on poverty; widespread poverty can sometimes lead to conflicts, state weakness, or state failure; state failure in turn can lead to mass migration; mass migration can cause stresses and security challenges in neighbouring states; and so on. But the more positive side of this inter-linkage for policy makers is that by tackling one non-traditional challenge, several potential threats to national security can be reduced. In this context, a study by the Wilson Center's Conflict Prevention Project gives the following examples:

> Engaging to reduce declining global health status would improve the quality of life for millions, increase faith in government service delivery, and reduce the drain on national incomes. Such cooperation might also facilitate diplomatic cooperation and discourse among tense allies. Similarly, a single intervention could address several threats. Universal access to non-sectarian education would improve countries' economic prospects, citizen faith in government, gender equity and health status.[469]

Another characteristic of most non-traditional threats is that they develop gradually – which does not mean that they cannot turn into urgent, if not catastrophic, threats some time in the future. The danger of these evolving long-term threats is that policy makers, often only thinking in terms of their four-year election cycle, may lack enough incentive to dedicate as many resources as necessary to prevent these long-term threats. The long-term nature of these threats can also be seen in a positive light, however: it allows for time to devise solid policies that may help prevent some of these threats, and for governments and societies to adapt to new circumstances.

The security challenges described above are extremely diverse. If all of them are going to be taken into account on their own, public officials run the risk of losing themselves in detail while failing to determine which threats or potential threats are the most urgent and lethal. Michael E. Brown suggests that security experts make "the problem of violent conflict" the "central issue on the security agenda".[470] Security experts should ask themselves how the many military and non-military challenges, both old and new, "can contribute to the *causes* of violent conflicts, including the most organized, most intense forms of violence – war and genocide".[471] The final chapter of this study embraces this forward-looking, prevention-oriented approach to security in its proposed NSC model. Before doing so, however, chapter 5 outlines a theoretical framework appropriate to the new security environment discussed above.

Chapter 5

New Approaches to Security and International Relations

The changed post-Cold War international security environment, which is characterised by the diverse and interconnected security challenges described in chapter 4, profoundly altered the dynamics of international relations. New frameworks and theories need to be worked out to better account for today's international environment and state interactions. Two previous and one forthcoming book by the author develop three innovative concepts on global security, international relations and cultural interactions in the 21st century.[472] The three concepts serve as an alternative to the "security dilemma" and zero-sum approaches to security developed by the realist school of international relations, which are no longer able to sufficiently describe today's globalising environment. The three concepts, which are briefly outlined in this chapter, are 1) the multi-sum security principle, multidimensionality and multilateralism; 2) symbiotic realism; and 3) transcivilizational synergy. They constitute the three conceptual pillars on which any sustainable national security strategy in the 21st century must rest.

1. The Five Dimensions of Global Security and the Multi-sum Security Principle[473]

As is discussed in chapter 2, the post-Cold War and post-11 September 2001 security doctrines of both the United States and the EU suggest that states are moving away from the rather narrow, traditional national security framework that has dominated national security thinking since the emergence of the modern nation state system in the 17th century. This framework supposed that if a state is secure from external threats and able to maintain law and order internally, individual citizens will automatically be protected from harm. As numerous historical examples illustrate, however, the sad truth is that this is not necessarily the case. In some states, the human rights of citizens are being violated by the very government that is supposed to protect them. Moreover, citizens of sovereign states can become victims of transnational threats that are beyond the ability of any individual government to eliminate. Cases in point are deadly attacks perpetrated by international terrorist groups or infection by a pandemic.

Until recently, national security has been concerned with defending and maintaining the territorial integrity of an individual state, while international security organisations were concerned with maintaining the integrity of the international state system. Following the end of World War II, the UN system, based on the principle of collective security, helped to stabilise the international state system and to mitigate the negative effects of an essentially anarchic world through the creation of an impressive body of international legal norms and rules. However, the United Nations has remained a very conservative institution in many respects and has not moved away from its state-centric security paradigm.

After the end of the Cold War, a variety of other security issues, such as intra-state conflicts, illegal migration, intensified transnational criminal activity and environmental degradation, forced international security experts to broaden the scope of the international security concept. Unable to tackle these threats on their own or on a state-by-state basis, states started to take collective measures against security threats posed by various non-state actors. Political scientist Michael Mihalka, for instance, seeks to distinguish this type of multilateral action from the collective security principle, whereby states form alliances to defend themselves against other states. Instead, he uses the term "cooperative security" to "describe cases where states work together to deal with non-state threats and challenges".[474] In many ways, however, the cooperative security approach also remains state-centric as it perceives state units as the "victims" of these non-state security threats.

The state-centric approach to security turned out to be insufficient to promote the security of individuals in a globalised world. As an alternative to the national security approach, some states, such as Canada and some EU member states, have proposed that the primary referent object of security should no longer be the state but the individual human being. Rather than addressing security issues solely at the national and international levels, the human security approach focuses on the security concerns of individuals.[475] In other words, it puts the security and well-being of individual people above the security of state entities. As Canadian Foreign Minister Lloyd Axworthy put it in 2001:

> Hobbled by economic adversity, outrun by globalization, and undermined from within by bad governance, the capacity of some states to provide this protection has increasingly come into question. This incapacity is particularly obvious in war-torn societies. The state has, at times, come to be a major threat to its population's rights and welfare – or has been incapable of restraining the warlords or paramilitary – rather than serving as the protector of its people. This drives us to broaden the focus of security beyond the level of the state and toward individual human beings, as well as to consider appropriate roles for the international system to compensate for state failure.[476]

The human security approach is certainly a big step forward in more effectively addressing security challenges in the 21st century.

As is noted in an earlier work, however, a focus on the state (national security) or on the individual (human security) does not grasp all the dimensions of the security challenges in an interconnected and interdependent world.[477] Besides focusing on the individual and the state, the need to protect the integrity of cultural and civilizational entities, as well as the need to promote peaceful interactions between these collective identities, must also be factored into the security equation (transcivilizational security). After all, there exist many collective entities that do not correspond with state borders; instead, they may span several states or form smaller communities within states.[478] Hence:

> The identification of the security of groups and cultures within states is particularly important within the context of transnational realities, including migration and irregular immigration and xenophobic and exclusionary tendencies in host societies with regard to culture, political beliefs, and religion. A better understanding of different cultures and greater tolerance and respect for diversity could help to...mitigate some of the most pressing security concerns of our day.[479]

As is discussed in chapter 4, clashes between different cultures strongly affect international security; thus, it makes sense to study cultural communities as independent entities. Cultural communities whose way of life is under threat need different kinds of protection to state entities, while violence perpetrated by members of cultural communities poses a different set of challenges to state aggression. Promoting better understanding and cooperation between cultures and civilizations (transcivilizational synergy) in turn will significantly enhance long-term global security.[480]

Another important security dimension involves transnational threats caused by any kind of illegal cross-border movements (transnational security). These threats are discussed in greater detail in chapter 4. Unlike the threat to territorial integrity posed by conquering state armies, transnational security threats for the most part threaten the political, social and economic integrity of states. The primary agents of these threats are non-state actors. Hence, state-based security arrangements no longer suffice to tackle these threats.

Finally, the protection of the natural habitat is another vital security dimension that needs to be dealt with on its own (environmental security). As is discussed in chapter 4, natural disasters – human-induced or not – and environmental pollution and degradation threaten the lives of individuals, the stability of states, and national and regional economies. These developments may lead to massive refugee flows and increased intra-state and interstate conflict. Environmental security thus constitutes a fifth key dimension of security today.

A modern conception of global security needs to include all five security dimensions: human, environmental, national, transnational and transcultural, all of which are included in the multi-sum security principle proposed in an earlier work.[481] The premise that underlines this new security concept is that the principle of justice needs to be applied to improve security in all five dimensions, because many security challenges are either directly or indirectly caused by injustice. In particular, real or perceived injustice can spawn feelings of humiliation, frustration and anger, which in some form or another can translate into violence. Injustice can make people feel alienated from their government and the rest of society, and some people as a result may be tempted to engage in illegal and/or violent acts to try to redress injustices.[482]

Injustice in the global sphere includes "a range of issues from the gap between rich and poor to the vulnerability of people to abuse, violence, occupation, exclusion, humiliation, disease, and starvation".[483] Finding fair solutions to redress these problems will make the world more secure. Global security can only be enhanced if the principle of justice guides the security policies of states, international agreements and post-conflict settlements.[484] Common rules and ethical guidelines based on justice constrain state behaviour and mitigate the effects of international anarchy caused by the lack of a global government.

Taking into account the new global environment, as well as the underlying importance of justice in creating a more secure world, the multi-sum security principle suggests that five security dimensions need to be taken into account.[485] Figure 1 below illustrates these five dimensions.

Figure 1: The Five Dimensions of Global Security and the Multi-sum Security Principle (*with permission from* LIT)[486]

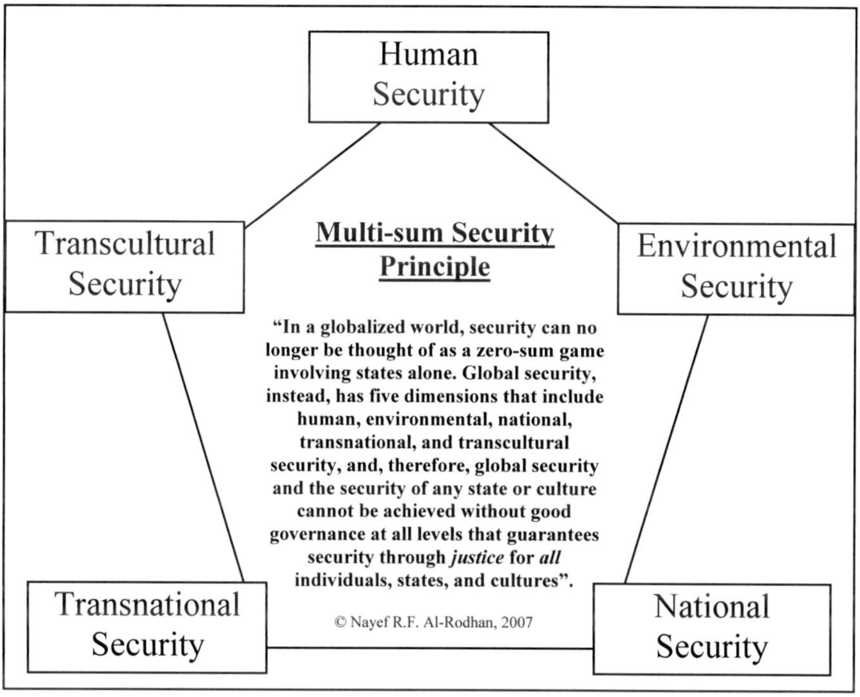

The application of the justice concept to the five dimensions of security has several manifestations. First, in the area of human security, it is important that national governments and international institutions do everything in their power to meet people's basic needs and eliminate severe poverty. Governments need to promote social justice by giving people equal opportunities in education and employment, as well as equal access to resources.[487] In post-conflict situations, human security can be maintained by building a just post-war order. Only if previously hostile parties to the conflict perceive the post-conflict settlement as fair and just will they be able to live together in peace and safety. Rather than focusing on punishment and revenge, post-conflict settlements would do better to promote reconciliation, such as through truth and reconciliation commissions.[488]

Second, in the area of environmental security, the concept of justice can trigger several conclusions. It may be argued that states and individual consumers owe it to future generations to protect the environment and thus use non-renewable natural resources sparingly.[489] Or, one might argue that the environment has its own intrinsic value and is not "owned" by humans but shared with many other living organisms. Hence, this implies a moral obligation on our part to take care of the natural environment.[490] Moreover, it is often the case that the poorest parts of the world suffer the most from environmental pollution and degradation. Poor developing countries often cannot afford newer and less-polluting technology for industrial production and power generation – and they can hardly impose and enforce stricter environmental laws on their fledgling economies. Moreover, poverty can force states to opt for short-term economic gains by depleting their own, non-renewable natural resources, such as through deforestation. In addition, developing countries currently seem to be hit hardest by the consequences of climate change – droughts in Africa and floods in some parts of Asia are cases in point. Hence, justice in the area of environmental security implies an obligation by wealthy nations, which are using up the vast majority of the world's resources and are also the world's greatest polluters, to fight global warming, invest in cleaner technologies, assist developing states to improve their environmental standards, and work towards increased global economic equality.

Third, in the area of national security, the justice concept has an important role to play in the spheres of politics and political economy. Only governments that govern justly will enjoy popular legitimacy and thus be stable and able to ensure law and order and effectively protect the homeland and their citizens. All this is best ensured by a government that represents the people of a state equally and contains sufficient checks and balances to prevent the abuse of power. Moreover, it is important that a government has an impartial and effective judicial system. This also implies that law enforcement must respect fundamental human rights and civil liberties. Incidentally, the national integrity of a state can be compromised if other states feel the need to intervene to stop human rights abuses. Finally, governments need to ensure that access to the country's resources is equal and that public goods are distributed fairly among the population. A fair taxation system and social security provisions will lead to more social justice.[491] Governments that govern according to principles of justice are unlikely to be overturned from within and will have enough citizen allegiance to be able to mobilize armies to protect the country's borders.

Fourth, in the area of transnational security, increased international justice will eliminate many of the causes of and incentives for illegal and violent activities inside states and across international borders. A case in point is international terrorism. Although any act of terrorism is completely unacceptable, regardless of the cause, the recruitment of terrorists is often facilitated if a terrorist group can appeal to a people's sense of injustice – be it due to political oppression, lack of economic opportunity, or some form of discrimination. To promote enhanced transnational security, states would thus need to take a two-pronged approach: there would need to be close international cooperation in the area of law-enforcement and intelligence sharing to catch terrorists and bring them to justice; and the international community would need to address some of the social, economic and political causes that lead some individuals to join terrorist organisations. Promoting increased global economic and social justice and helping states to institute good governance are some of the measures that can be taken to ensure long-term transnational security.[492]

Fifth, transcultural security implies the absence of hostile clashes between members of different cultures. The application of justice to this area means rooting out discrimination on the basis of nationality, religion or ethnicity around the world. Promoting better cultural understanding in countries with different cultural communities (including immigrant communities) is one way of preventing the demonisation of one group by another based on rumours and misinformation.[493] All in all, the multi-sum security principle puts forward a framework that identifies the diversity of phenomena that affect the security of individuals, states and cultures.

2. Symbiotic Realism[494]

Realism is currently the dominant perspective in international relations, but it is hardly a single theory. It is based on a set of assumptions according to which states are rational and unitary actors. The goal of a state is to maximise its national interest, and the accumulation and exercise of power is the key to understanding international behaviour. Classical realists define state interests in strictly material terms and explain policy change as a result of the changing distribution of power, particularly military and economic power. For realists, military power remains the most effective means of ensuring national security and state survival. For this reason, the military distribution of power continues to be essential. State sovereignty is everything to the realists because the international system is state-centric and states are considered to be the key actors in international relations.

Realists see power politics as a zero-sum game whereby the only way in which states can increase their power is by taking it away from others. Realists maintain that, in the absence of an overarching authority structure, states will more or less behave like individuals in the anarchical state of nature described by Hobbes. That is, states are essentially left to fend for themselves, are unable to trust each other and, if they want to survive, egoistically have to look after their own safety – often at the expense of others. In the Hobbesian world, gains are relative, that is, more security for one state entails less security for another.

It is true that during the Cold War, realism seemed to provide a fairly accurate description of the international environment. States, when engaged in national security policy making, primarily concentrated on potential military conflicts between states. However, there is a debate among foreign policy theorists about whether today's international environment, where transnational forces and actors are increasingly dominant, can still be accurately described using the realist framework.

Realists today argue that the end of the Cold War and the process of globalisation have not changed the basis of the international system. After all, the international system is still based on state units. Moreover, its anarchic character has remained in place because there is not yet a world government. Hence, states will continue to have to look after themselves to ensure their physical security. Realists argue that relations between states, including competition for power and influence, will continue to dominate international relations in the 21st century.[495]

Political theorists critical of realism contend that the international system is currently undergoing changes that will have a decisive impact on the way states conduct security policy. They maintain that economic globalisation and the information revolution are decisively changing power relationships not just between states but also between governments and other actors, including international corporations and non-state actors.[496] Hence, simply concentrating on state entities' pursuit of maximising their power does not give an accurate picture of the world we live in.

Nonetheless, the basic structure of the international system has remained the same. As Michael Brown observes, the realist paradigm still provides an accurate description of the basic structure: "The international system is still anarchic; states are still the dominant actors in international relations; states still seek security; and interstate security competitions and confrontations will continue to be important features of the security landscape".[497] At the same time, globalisation constitutes a powerful force that undermines state power, empowers non-state actors and brings with it new security threats that come from sources other than conventional state armies.

The book *Symbiotic Realism: A Theory of International Relations in an Instant and an Interdependent World* suggests that students of international relations today need to consider at least nine different actors and dynamic factors that have an impact on the international system. They are the individual, women, the state, large collective entities, international organisations, transnational corporations, the environment, natural resources, and information and communications technology.[498] Note the addition of the environment and natural resources as independent dynamic factors. The environment and natural resources are "reactive actors" and a "non-conscious form of agency". They are relevant as part of today's interactive global system in the sense that they are "reacting to human activities in such a way as to call into question current levels of civilization and to transform aspects of the global system, for example, through climate change".[499]

Large collective entities refers to groups of people that share a common identity based on a shared culture, religion, ethnicity or ideological commitment. A case in point are cultural entities at the sub-national or supranational level, which, due to increased connectivity, interdependence and human mobility, deal with each other and have to manage their coexistence at an unprecedented level. The dynamics between large collective entities have a significant impact on the global system. From neurobiology, it is known that humans have an innate desire to form their sense of identity from being part of a larger group or entity. This human drive can lead to several consequences with an impact on the international system. It can lead to cultural arrogance and exceptionalism among particular entities, or the dissolution of a collective entity, for whatever reason, can lead to a sense of disorientation among former group members. All these outcomes can lead to increased insecurity and potential conflicts.[500]

Symbiotic realism posits that "synergy should be the guiding principle in the search for better ways to manage culturally pluralistic societies and relations between civilizations".[501] Through transcivilizational synergy, cultural entities are able to achieve more than they could on their own. It is a necessary prerequisite to find better solutions for many of the 21st century's complex challenges. Ultimately, however, synergy among the world's cultures can be a result of the globalisation process, instant communication and increased human mobility, leading to the creation of a global cultural superstructure based on common values.

The theory goes beyond realism, which focuses almost exclusively on state actors and self-help, and takes into account the new global circumstances of multiple actors. The theory accepts the realist description of the international environment as being essentially anarchic, but adds three other dynamics that characterise the global system of today. These are instant connectivity, interdependence and the predilections of human nature.

Instant connectivity refers to the notion that due to new ICT, such as the Internet and satellite television, information can be exchanged and spread among the most far-flung corners of the world within minutes. This fundamentally changes international relations. In particular, governments are no longer in full control of information that can affect national and international security or diplomatic relationships between states. Instead, they often find themselves in a position where they have to react to information spread by news agencies. Symbiotic realism attempts to account for the relative decline in the power of states as the determining agents of international interactions. The theory sees states as only one part of the multiplicity of actors setting the global agenda today.

Today's strong interdependence among individual state units is also accounted for in the theory of symbiotic realism, which recognises the many common interests among states today. The theory thus modifies the realist claim that international politics is a zero-sum game where states vie for power by taking it away from others. In an interdependent world, it is indeed possible for a state to become stronger not at the expense of others, but by having other states benefit from its increased strength. Symbiotic realism thus emphasises absolute gains as opposed to relative gains.

Indeed, states today depend on others to increase their national security. The ability of some states to bring non-state-based threats under control will enhance the security of other states affected by the same problems. Hence, the notion of a symbiosis: states, as rational actors, often act in ways in which they try to benefit from each other by cooperating constructively with others. If one state is able to increase its strength, for example, through rapid economic development, other states can benefit through increased trade. Large military powers, if they comply with international norms and do not display aggressive behaviour, do not automatically trigger the formation of countervailing alliances. Instead, strong powers should be able to accommodate the interests of weaker states. International relations can therefore no longer be looked at as a zero-sum game, but as a set of interactions where absolute gains are possible, even if not common.

The theory of symbiotic realism recognises that a state's power can also come in part from the values and norms that the state promotes as well as its hard power capabilities. This multi-dimensional view of power can thus better account for the fact that although there currently are attempts by states to balance out US dominance, these attempts are much more modest than realist balance of power theories would predict.[502] Many states today perceive the United States not as a threat, but as protection from other threats that they fear more. Shared interests as a result of interdependence between the United States and other states distract from the large military imbalance that exists between them. A hegemony based on consent can make up for the lack of a world government and mitigate the negative effects of global anarchy.[503]

Furthermore, the theory takes into account the predilections of human nature. It shares (but also goes beyond) the basic realist assumption that humans are driven by the desire to fulfil their basic human needs, including food, shelter and personal safety. Moreover, the theory identifies fear as an important motivating factor that can lead to the aggressive pursuit of power and attempts to dominate others. While human beings may be egoistical and ruthless until they can live in safety, they are capable of ethical behaviour once these needs are met.[504] Symbiotic realism uses the neurobiological conception of human nature, which states that the human ego is not simply preoccupied with the pursuit of power and domination, but also strives for a sense of belonging and a positive identity.[505] Perceptions, and not just material capabilities, can thus equally motivate state behaviour.[506]

The implications of this theory for policy making are manifold. Considering the strong influence that ICT has on today's international system, some better ways to regulate the flow of information might need to be found. Such regulatory mechanisms should not compromise free speech and reduce access to information, but prevent the large-scale spread of harmful and false information. Similarly, supranational bodies would need to regulate transnational corporations and enforce their transparency.[507] Furthermore, states and international organisations need to work together to promote sustainable development and stop environmental degradation. Besides implementing international environmental regulations, state and private investment in the development of new, "clean" technologies is equally important. Technological innovation will also help to reduce resource scarcities that may lead to conflicts among global actors.[508]

National governments would need to protect human rights and the rights of groups effectively, including rights guaranteeing a minimum standard of living. The concept of human security comes in here, which involves "the absence of hunger and illness, respect for human rights and dignity, as well as the absence of violence and armed conflict that typically have a huge impact on civilian populations".[509] Special attention should be paid to women's rights, taking into account the needs and concerns affecting women specifically, including the promotion of gender equality and granting women reproductive rights.[510] Focusing on human security by striving to make people's lives more secure will decrease tensions among individuals and collective entities, which ultimately enhances the national security and overall stability of state units and with it the global state system.

Symbiotic realism suggests that relations between states are to be characterised by increasing levels of mutual dependence, where one state can make individual gains without weakening others or causing insecurity. Hence, absolute gains are possible, and creating balances of power becomes unnecessary. In an essentially anarchic international system, it is up to international organisations to promote a more just and environmentally sustainable global order.

At the inter-civilizational level, the world's major civilizations have a large role to play in promoting international peace and improving the global order if their relations are "guided by the principle of synergy, which implies that a plurality of civilizations will have a larger net effect than any one civilization alone". [511] Through mutual borrowing and exchanges, different cultures and civilizations will be able to improve the quality of social energy necessary to face the challenges posed by our interconnected world. Taken together, symbiotic realism promotes a comprehensive vision of the dimensions and dynamics of today's interconnected world.

3. Transcivilizational Synergy[512]

Looking at the history of some of the world's most prominent civilizations, the significance of cross-civilizational fertilisation in their development cannot be overemphasised. A previous work by the author has cited numerous examples of historically significant inter-cultural exchanges. For instance, the development of modern European culture was strongly aided by Arab influences, especially in terms of Arab cultural, scientific and technical contributions.[513] In fact, cultural entities would become stagnant and ossified without these kinds of exchanges.[514]

Cross-fertilisation is necessary for cultures to remain vibrant, and globalisation must promote this process. It is important to make sure that what sometimes are referred to as cultural or civilizational "clashes" become fruitful exchanges: "Exchanges would not only increase awareness of each other and, thereby, promote mutual recognition; [they] would also help to deal with the multitude of challenges faced in relation to globalization".[515] With all the complex security problems humans face today, there is a great need for cultural and scientific creativity to tackle them – creativity that can be fostered and greatly enhanced through cross-cultural exchanges: "The notion of synergy implies that a plurality of cultures can have a net effect that is greater than the impact of the efforts of members of any one culture alone".[516]

Transcultural and transcivilizational synergy is a vital building block of international stability and peace. Synergy is achieved when a new global collective consciousness is formed, a consciousness that is based on mutual respect and the conviction that diversity in belief, culture and language is "a source of strength and creativity".[517] Co-existence, not cultural homogenisation, thus needs to be nurtured. Peaceful co-existence between different civilizations can only be sustained through increased global justice, especially in the spheres of economics and trade. Consequently, transcivilizational synergy "depends upon empowering diversity through fair competition for the betterment of humanity".[518]

This chapter has outlined a theoretical framework within a comprehensive description of the security environment and international relations in the 21st century. Figure 2 below illustrates this framework in the shape of an octagon. The multi-sum security principle states that global security today consists of five dimensions: the human, environmental, national, transnational and transcultural security dimensions. To achieve global harmony, all five security spheres need to be governed justly by respecting the rights and well-being of individuals, states, cultural communities and the environment. Hence, the notion of multi-dimensionality: genuine, long-lasting global security can only be achieved by respecting all five security dimensions. International relations in the 21st century thus can no longer be seen as a zero-sum game between states but rather as an interconnected, multidimensional web where gains in one security sphere will affect successes and failures in other security spheres, and the gains of one state can lead to gains in other states.

The symbiotic realism principle describes the different actors that dominate international politics today. These actors are the individual, women, the state, large collective entities, international organisations, transnational corporations, the environment, natural resources and ICT. According to symbiotic realism, four features characterise the 21st century global environment: anarchy, instant connectivity, interdependence and the predilections of human nature. The nine different actors influence and are influenced in one way or another by the four dynamics that characterise the international system. The result of this web of dynamics is symbiosis: the notion that the different foreign policy actors can benefit from one another, and that the gains of one actor do not necessarily imply losses for another actor. Transnational interactions between different cultures and civilizations will eventually lead to transcivilizational synergy, whereby different cultural entities merge and jointly are able to achieve more than they would on their own.

The long-term security of states in the 21st century thus rests on three pillars. These are 1) the *multi-sum security principle* (a prescription for global security based on justice, multidimensionality and multilateralism); 2) *symbiotic realism* (a prescription for conducting international relations in an interdependent world where absolute gains are possible); and 3) *transcivilizational synergy* (a prescription for dealing with collective sub-national and supranational entities). The three concepts naturally give rise to a new national security framework, one that takes the multiplicity of actors and security dimensions into account and recognises the need for multilateral cooperation and transcivilizational synergy. Such a framework is outlined in chapter 6.

Figure 2: Sustainable National Security in a Transnational World

* N.R.F. Al-Rodhan, *The Five Dimensions of Global Security: Proposal for a Multi-sum Security Principle* (Berlin: LIT Verlag, 2007)

** N.R.F. Al-Rodhan, *Symbiotic Realism: A Theory of International Relations in an Instant and an Interdependent World* (Berlin: LIT Verlag, 2007).

*** N.R.F. Al-Rodhan, *Transcivilizational Synergy* (working title), *forthcoming*, 2008.

CHAPTER 6

A NEW NATIONAL SECURITY MODEL FOR THE 21ST CENTURY

Bold new thinking is required about national security. A national security framework for the 21st century needs to incorporate both old and new elements. States will have to continue to be concerned about their territorial integrity and the physical safety of their citizens, but they have to look beyond their immediate neighbourhood in order to effectively protect themselves and their citizens. States will continue to maintain national militaries for their own protection, but may also want to have people on staff able to contribute to state building projects abroad. States will continue to be concerned about the spread of diseases and environmental pollution at home, but they will also be required to monitor pathological and environmental developments around the world and to take preventative measures before the problem reaches their borders. In short, states today have to think in much more global and multidimensional terms than they used to.

In practical terms, the 21st century security environment requires states to take a plethora of issues and interrelationships into account when making security policy. This requires experts from very different fields to work together and consider the consequences of a particular threat or proposed state action in all the different security dimensions. It would thus be very useful for states to have access to an advisory body in the form of a national security council. As is noted above, the central task of a national security council is to pull together the security concerns, interests and security-related policy recommendations of the state's different government departments and security experts. It analyses the possible advantages and disadvantages of different policy recommendations and presents them to the leadership of the state, such as the president or prime minister. In doing so, the NSC is meant to act as a buffer or neutraliser of the different agendas pursued by the various government departments and prevents one single department from gaining the upper hand in determining security policy.

An ideal NSC seeks to objectively evaluate the departments' various concerns and include them in national security policy planning where appropriate. Members of the NSC thereby weigh the different security concerns of the departments against one another and prioritise them according to the overall interests of the state and its citizens. The NSC staff would then put forward its own national security policy recommendation with regard to what it considers to be the country's most urgent short- and long-term threats. In emergency situations, where immediate action is required, the council can serve as a panel of highly qualified people able quickly to provide relevant information and advice to the leader of the state.

A national security framework for the 21st century would reflect the six broad criteria for a successful national security strategy developed by the Princeton Project on National Security.[519] First, any approach to national security in the 21st century must be multidimensional. It must account for the breadth of traditional and non-traditional, intended and non-intended threats. One threat cannot be neglected at the expense of another which may at that moment seem more pressing. Second, any strategy must combine hard- and soft-power tools to neutralise threats. Soft power particularly involves a state's ability to win other states to its side through good communication and persuasion. Third, any successful national security strategy today is based on the recognition that going it alone is no longer feasible. Finding common security interests with other states and pursuing them together is the only way to enhance national security in the long term.

Fourth, states should adhere to universal values in their foreign policy. Only in this way is it possible to win long-term allies that share the same principles and to avoid hostile alliances. Nothing can bind states together more than the notion of jointly pursuing a larger goal. Fifth, what happens inside one state is of national security interest for other states. Weak domestic institutions, a developing civil war, the uncontrolled spread of an infectious disease and the breakdown of law and order inside one state pose threats to others. Part of a good national security policy of any state is thus the willingness to help other states solve their internal problems and become stable again. Sixth, any national security strategy needs to adjust to the new information age. This means that states need to be highly flexible in their policies and able to react quickly to changing circumstances caused by the rapid spread of new information. Dealing with vast amounts of information and distinguishing the true from the false is another capability that states need to develop.[520]

The information age has fundamentally changed the way strategic planning needs to be approached. Daniel M. Gerstein, a former Military Fellow at the Council on Foreign Relations, explains: "Strategy has been defined as the linking of *ways* and *means* to achieve *ends* while mitigating *risks*. In the future, we must factor *environment* into any reasonable discussion of strategy [italics in original]".[521] He goes on, "Ends, ways, and means all apply to the country developing the strategy", and all these aspects of strategy are "owned" by the state developing it.[522] By including environment in the equation, Gerstein accounts for the fact that an important aspect of executing any strategy in the information age is beyond the state's control, but will have a decisive impact on the relative success or failure of the strategy. With environment, Gerstein seeks to include factors such as the way other states perceive and react to the strategy, and whether a particular goal pursued in another state – say, peacebuilding troops trying to form a democratic government – is feasible considering the circumstances.[523]

In the information age, any strategy pursued by a state is under constant public scrutiny. Other states, journalists, bloggers, NGOs and other non-state actors can make their opinions and critique of the policy heard and spread it instantaneously through the Internet and/or the global media, so a state cannot achieve the desired ends without taking into account the way its policy is portrayed and perceived by others. If a policy comes under widespread public criticism around the world, a state will need to respond to it by trying to explain the rationale behind the policy better or by making necessary adjustments. Because state actions today are under intense public scrutiny, states become less flexible in their actions, and leaders are becoming more accountable for their decisions.[524]

Ideally, a national security council would be able to draw on experts on a broad range of issues. As Figure 3 suggests, an ideal national security council may consist of a Board, supported by several Issue Groups and Principles and Future Trajectories Divisions. The former would be concerned with different security-related issues, the latter would oversee policy processes, hold individual policy decisions up against universal standards and think about future contingencies. It is important that members of the NSC work in close proximity to each other to facilitate informal meetings and discussions among staff members. As one study of the US NSC process found, "The results and agreements reached through personal discussions are not always formally reported, but this networking is an important lubricant for the national security process at large".[525]

The role of an NSC should be that of an honest, independent broker able to reconcile the interests of the different government departments and ministries. The collectively agreed policy recommendations of the NSC board should trump any attempt by an individual department – that might be represented by a strong personality – to monopolise a particular policy issue, subdue opposing views, or convince the country's leader that the proposed departmental policy is the only viable policy option. A security council is supposed to avoid exactly that. Instead, the council's policy recommendations must reflect the different views and concerns voiced by the different members of the NSC in a balanced way and take them into account equally. The NSC will act on the instructions of the elected government leadership to come up with security policy proposals and draft analyses of potential future security threats. In addition, the NSC is tasked with monitoring international events and bringing these to the attention of the government, which may in turn ask the NSC to analyse theses issues further.

1. The NSC Board

The NSC Board in the model in Figure 3 is headed by the president or prime minister's national security adviser, whose task it is to educate the country's leader about the available security policy options worked out by NSC staff members. During NSC meetings, the national security adviser plays the role of honest broker between the different departmental standpoints represented in the NSC. The president or prime minister may attend NSC meetings at any time. The Board also includes the representatives of various cabinet-level government departments and relevant government organisations, including intelligence, environmental and other agencies as applicable. In addition, the Board includes the heads of the Issue Groups and the Principles and Future Trajectories Divisions. The members of the Board work together to share information and coordinate the

Figure 3: National Security Council Structure for Sustainable National Security in a Transnational World

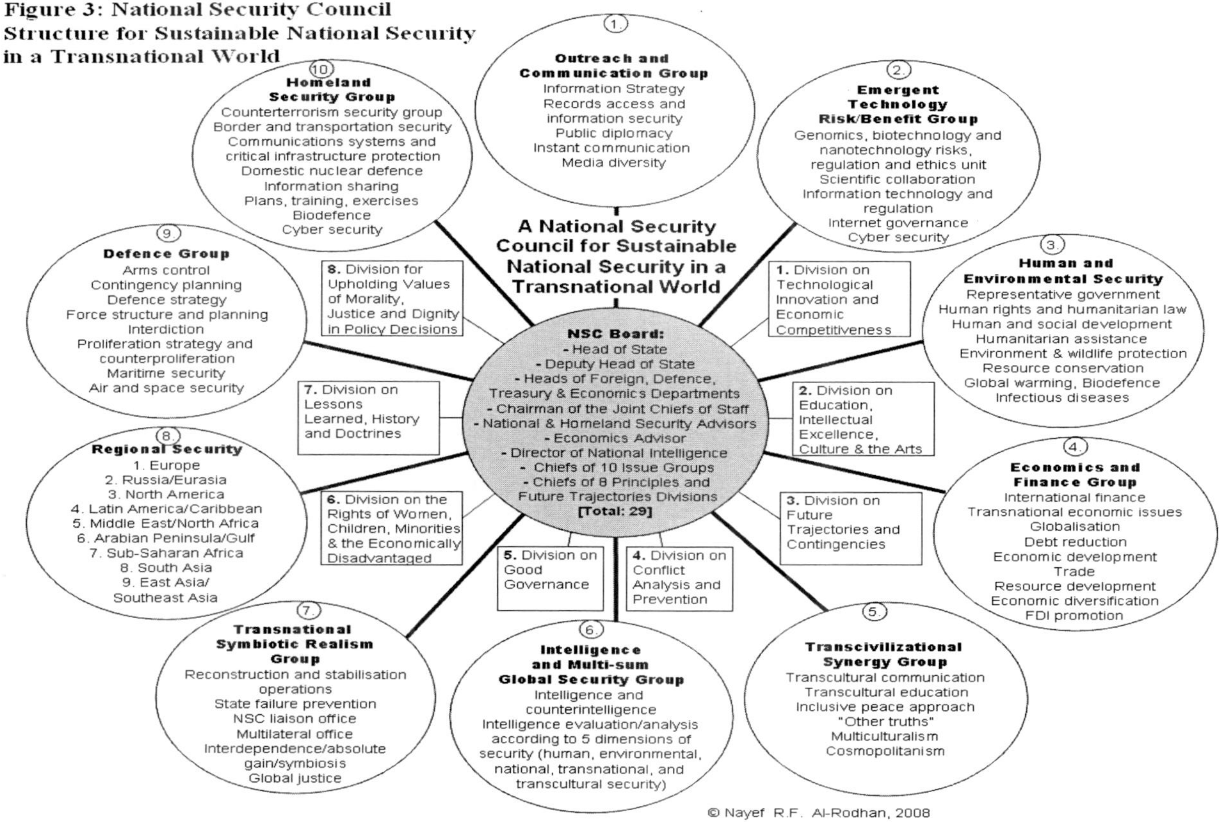

implementation of security policy among the different government departments.

2. Issue Groups

Issue Groups cover a broad range of areas where security-related challenges can emerge. There are ten different issues that in one way or another need to be addressed by any modern national security council. The numbering below corresponds with the circled numbers in Figure 3.

1. Outreach and Communication Group
States today are under constant public scrutiny. In the information age, the way in which a government communicates its policies at home and abroad has an impact on the ultimate success of these policies. Government policies are widely debated and criticised on global television networks as well as on Internet news sites and blogs. Every national security council today has to take this new environment into account.

A state can no longer simply decide to do A in order to achieve B and then single-mindedly pursue the policy to the end. B cannot be achieved if there is widespread international resistance to strategy A, which can damage the credibility and ultimately compromise the security of the state pursuing the policy. Achieving B might still be the right goal to enhance the security of the state, but due to widespread international opposition, the state might have to modify strategy A and come up with a better way of achieving B. Communication is therefore key: a state whose policies are under intense public scrutiny and analysed and debated on global communications outlets in real time has to have good means to communicate and explain its policy to the public. If a state fails to do so, it can be sure that others will, and they may intentionally or unintentionally distort the conduct and rationale of the policy pursued. The Outreach and Communication Group is charged with devising a communications strategy accompanying the execution of the country's security policy. In addition, the group may be involved in outreach programmes to engage in a dialogue with people from other cultures inside and outside the country in order to foster inter-cultural understanding and synergies.

The purpose of this group is not to become a propaganda machine for the government. Laws that ensure government transparency and freedom of the press should be able to prevent this. Instead, the group would be staffed by politically impartial, media-savvy experts able to understand the security implications of the information age. The group addresses potential dangers connected to new ways of mass communications, such as blogs. Blogs, if unregulated, can be a means to spread messages of hate very quickly. The division would thus draft policy recommendations, including ethical guidelines for bloggers and proposals for laws banning blogs engaged in defamation and the promotion of criminal activity.[526]

2. Emergent Technology Risk/Benefit Group

Genomics, biotechnology and nanotechnology are promising new fields in the natural sciences that open the door to revolutionary technological inventions. This group is concerned with the ways in which these new technologies may help to enhance human security and well-being, as well as with the potential dangers these technologies may pose to human health and security. Both biotechnology and nanotechnology have huge potentials to improve human security and well-being around the world. The new technologies can help to dramatically increase crop yields and improve the quality and nutritional content of food plants and livestock. Biologically engineered bacteria and plants can help to remove organic waste and heavy metals from drinking water.[527] Biotechnology further holds out the promise of the development of new vaccines. Moreover, the technology can be used to develop strategies to deplete or incapacitate insects capable of transmitting human diseases.[528]

Considering that hunger and poverty are the main catalysts for instability, extremism and violence, it is in the national security interests of those nations with advanced technological know-how in these areas to share their knowledge with less advanced states.

Of course, this group will also be concerned with possible misuses of these technologies. In the defence sector, it is important to keep up with the new technologies to prevent the state from falling back in the global balance of power. Nanotechnology and biotechnology might soon be successfully employed in warfare. As for nanotechnology, new offensive capabilities might include “Smaller, more efficient weapons, including energy weapons; greater use of robotics; hypersonic missiles and jets”, and so on.[529]

At the same time, states will need to do everything in their power to prevent a new arms race based on the new technologies from occurring. A large part of this group’s work would thus involve cooperation with scientists and representatives from other states to come up with a verifiable regime that limits the use of these technologies for weapons purposes. As one study suggests, "The establishment of an organization for the Prohibition of Biological Weapons modelled after the IAEA could well provide the platform for a global bargain of making technology available for development while protecting its misuse."[530]

The danger that terrorists might acquire some of these emerging technologies and engineer deadly weapons for use against civilian targets is also a major fear. Although the use of nanotechnology by terrorists is deemed unlikely in the short and medium term, because the technology is very high-tech,[531] biotechnology is more likely to be employed by terrorist groups. The use of biological weapons against humans, livestock and plants can have disastrous consequences. Security councils around the world need to be aware of and prepare for the possibility of such attacks. Biotechnology can be employed to build highly sensitive sensors to detect biological attacks early and neutralise deadly agents before they can spread.[532]

In sum, the Emergent Technology Risk/Benefit Group would pursue two goals: first, to share and promote the legitimate use of these new sciences around the world, as these technologies can help to massively improve human security; and, second, to support the creation of an international regime to counter the misuse of these technologies by hostile states and terrorist groups.

3. Human and Environmental Security Group

This group, staffed with people with a background in biology, epidemiology and the medical sciences, is concerned with human health and the environment. It closely studies and tracks infectious diseases at home and abroad. It devises measures to protect the population at home (such as through vaccinations and the stockpiling of medication). Moreover, it proposes ways to help those countries where infectious diseases are spreading fastest to contain them. This group will have to pay particular attention to states with a weak government and health infrastructure, as infectious diseases in such states often remain undetected and quickly spread beyond control. A particular long-term concern of this group is the HIV/AIDS epidemic in Asia and Africa, which continues to cause indescribable human suffering and hampers economic development in many countries.

The group is also concerned with the health of the natural environment, which is strongly connected to human health issues. For instance, industrial contamination of rivers and ground water can lead to all sorts of health problems in humans; and the same fossil fuels that are believed to cause global warming also negatively affect human health. The expected consequences of global warming, such as floods and droughts, also pose dangers to the health and lives of humans. The group would suggest policies to protect the environment at home and work with other countries and at the UN to devise binding international treaties that tackle global environmental problems, including air pollution and global warming.

The group also deals with more long-term issues to promote human well-being through human and social development both at home and abroad. Education about healthy nutrition and disease prevention is one key aspect. Moreover, helping poor countries to develop a better health service infrastructure is a fairly inexpensive way of improving global security. As the World Health Organization's Commission on Macroeconomics and Health estimates, "in the poorer developing countries, better health services, including a few specific interventions against infectious diseases and better nutrition could save up to 8 million lives per year by 2010."[533] This, of course, implies that increased investment in health would lead to considerable economic growth. It is thus crucial that security councils make the health of both human beings and the environment an integral objective of overall security policy.

4. Economics and Finance Group

This group is concerned with the state of the national and the global economy. As domestic economies today are so strongly integrated with the global economy, the group will need to focus on both at the same time. Working with other states to stabilise the global economy serves important security interests, bearing in mind that economic crises often lead to political instability. For developing countries, attracting high quality foreign direct investment (FDI) is an important aspect of building solid economic foundations. It was shown in the former communist countries of Eastern Europe that FDI can raise productivity levels and living standards considerably.[534] Moreover, states that are heavily dependent on a single export commodity have to be concerned with promoting diversification, so that resource depletion or a sudden decline in the world market price for this commodity does not plunge the country into an economic crisis. Countries with economies that are highly dependent on the export of primary commodities have been shown to be at much higher risk of violent internal conflict than other poor countries, especially in those times when commodity prices fall.[535]

5. Transcivilizational Synergy Group

This group is concerned with an important aspect of the theory of symbiotic realism – developed in an earlier work and summarised in chapter five.[536] It works towards the goal of achieving transcivilizational synergy. To recapitulate, transcivilizational synergy refers to the joining together of the world's cultures and civilizations, whereby these different groups exchange and merge the richness of their respective cultural knowledge and insights in an effort to work together and find common solutions to the world's problems. Every national security council in the world should have people on staff who contribute to this process. Inside the country, the group makes policy recommendations to improve cultural understanding and foster social peace and cohesion. Furthermore, the group ensures that the country's foreign policy is not infused with cultural arrogance, but promotes tolerance and displays a high level of cultural sensitivity.

This group would also give advice to the Outreach and Communication Group on how a particular national security strategy can best be communicated to people from different cultures. This becomes especially important in the information age, where people around the world can see and interpret a state's policy in real time.[537] This group can use its knowledge about other cultures to make educated guesses about how a new policy will be received and interpreted by other cultures around the world and give advice about how the rationale of the policy can best be communicated. Based on the notion of multiple truths, the group would take into account that other cultures do not see a particular action in the same way as we think we would if we were in the same situation. The ability to understand others on their own terms rather than seeing them as mirror images of us is crucial in today's global environment.

6. Intelligence and Multi-sum Global Security Group

This group is concerned with evaluating incoming intelligence about the whole range of security threats that affect states today. It serves as the hub for intelligence analysis, where all relevant information from national and foreign intelligence agencies, as well as open-source information, is brought together and analysed. The group faces the challenge of making sure that threats in all five dimensions of global security, as identified by the multi-sum security principle, are taken into account. The five dimensions include human, environmental, national, transnational and transcultural security. The group also ensures that objective measures are applied when determining which of the potential threats identified by the intelligence community should be dealt with most urgently.

7. Transnational Symbiotic Realism Group

International politics in the 21st century is not a zero-sum game. Instead, states are mutually dependent on each other for their own national security. The success of one state – say, in the sphere of economic development or domestic law enforcement – can benefit other states. In other words, absolute gains are possible in 21st century international relations. The Transnational Symbiotic Realism Group studies the ways in which different security policy options affect the five dimensions of security identified by the multi-sum security principle.

In an interconnected world, simply pursuing one's short-term national interest is not a wise basis for national security policy making. Today, it is very easy for states to win all the battles but lose the war. A state may pursue and achieve all its national interest objectives, but end up less secure and less strong if, by pursuing its policies, it has alienated its allies and world public opinion. The Transnational Symbiotic Realism Group promotes the idea that national security today cannot be achieved by making others feel less secure. As Gerstein suggests, "if there are decisions that are in the near-term perhaps less than optimal for [a state's] interests, but will collectively provide greater benefit to allies or globally" it might nevertheless be worthwhile for a state to go along with the policy.[538]

The Transnational Symbiotic Realism Group ensures that the national security policies pursued by the state do not compromise the security of other states. It makes sure that the concerns and interests of other states are taken into account.

Furthermore, the group verifies that national security policies do not violate international laws and norms. To achieve a more orderly global system, it is important that states observe international norms and laws, which constrain state actions and thus dampen the negative effects of international anarchy. Especially in the information age, a state action that violates international norms is detrimental to the state's image and credibility, and thus weakens the state in the future.

Furthermore, the group maintains an NSC liaison office that stays in touch with NSCs in other countries and promotes transnational security cooperation. It also helps to coordinate the state's involvement in multilateral efforts around the world. Among those would be UN affairs and international humanitarian aid policy, as well as multilateral efforts to safeguard the environment and fight the spread of infectious diseases.

In short, the Transnational Symbiotic Realism Group ensures that the state pursues its national security interests by staying in constant dialogue with other states, based on the consideration that only mutual support of each others' security interests will improve the international security environment, and with it the security of the individual state.

8. Regional Security Group

In an interdependent world, it no longer makes sense to take a country-by-country approach. Instead, foreign policy towards one country needs to be coordinated with foreign policies pursued towards all other countries located in the same region. Most transnational threats can be attributed not to an individual country but to a problem that is afflicting an entire region. For example, the influx of large numbers of migrants from country X into country Y leads to civil violence and state instability in country Y. If an outside state now wants to help to stabilise country Y, it cannot do so without also tackling the problems that led to massive emigration from country X. By having national security experts concentrate on regional dynamics rather than specialising in a particular country, they are better able to see the whole picture, determine the root causes of a problem and find comprehensive solutions that benefit the entire region. The Regional Security Group would therefore have experts on every major region of the world on staff.

9. Defence Group

The Defence Group deals with traditional security threats, that is, hard-power threats emanating from other states. It identifies possible enemy states abroad and is concerned with the changing balance of hard-power capabilities. The Defence Group looks after contingency planning and equipping and training the country's armed forces to successfully neutralise possible attacks from other states. The Defence Group seeks to minimise potential new threats from states by participating in counterproliferation efforts, especially concerning WMD, because the acquisition of WMD by one state can shift the balance of power dramatically and might embolden a state to engage in adventurous policies. The Defence Group, in dealing with "traditional threats", builds on the state's long-term experience in defending its territorial integrity in time of war and peace.

10. Homeland Security Group
The Homeland Security Group, by its very definition, is concerned with securing the country's borders and protecting citizens from threats emanating from the inside. It designs appropriate strategies to protect the country's critical infrastructure, including transportation and communications networks, cyberspace, nuclear facilities, and so on. It also seeks to identify and neutralise terrorist groups at home. It would therefore need to work continuously on reconciling the tension between the imperative to protect citizens from harm while also respecting their civil liberties, such as their right to privacy and freedom of speech.

3. Principles and Future Trajectories Divisions

The Principles and Future Trajectories Divisions that appear in Figure 3 are concerned with more long-term security issues and try to address challenges before they turn into direct security threats. The divisions examine future contingencies, conflict analysis and the promotion of good governance, among other issues.

1. Division on Technological Innovation and Economic Competitiveness
Keeping up with the latest technologies is imperative for the long-term security of any state. Most important is a country's ability to integrate and apply new technologies, regardless of "whether the technologies are acquired through a country's own basic research or from technology leaders".[539] Since the 1990s, the technology to adopt and keep up with has been ICT. The so-called digital divide has left those countries and people that lack access to new technologies unable to compete in

the global economy. Economic underdevelopment, as stated several times, can lead to human misery and discontent, state instability and migration – to mention just a few security-related consequences.

Moreover, for a state to maintain its economic competitiveness, it needs to keep up with other new technologies as well, including genomics, biotechnology and nanotechnology. States also have an interest in supporting the promotion of technological innovations in the context of environmental security. The development and application of technologies that help to reduce the emission of greenhouse gasses and other pollutants, or that help to reduce a state's dependency on oil and gas imports, are clearly in the security interest of states. Considering the promising prospects for biotechnology and nanotechnology in tackling starvation, these technologies could help to dramatically increase the quality of life for people living in some of the world's poorest countries. Poor countries can support the application of these promising new technologies by pursuing policies in support of "good governance, universal education, and market reforms".[540] In short, the division, taking a more long-term view of national security, would work together with private industry to ensure that the country adopts new technologies either as a developer or consumer. In doing so, the division helps to promote sustained economic growth and increased human security through a better quality of life.

2. Division on Education, Intellectual Excellence, Culture and the Arts

This division is staffed with educational experts and academics in close contact with the government's education department. It is concerned with the security benefits reaped by promoting good, comprehensive educational institutions at home and abroad. Education might be one of the most powerful tools available to promote global peace and security.

As is noted above, states that fall behind in adopting and developing new technologies will see their national security, and above all their welfare, compromised. It is thus easy for most states to understand the importance of promoting science education as part of a comprehensive, long-term national security and economic strategy. However, in today's interconnected world, much more is needed in the educational sphere. Educational institutions play a key role in conveying values and teaching essential skills to future leaders and world citizens. Good training in the social sciences and humanities is important to keep democracies thriving and exposing people to different ideas and cultures. From a national security perspective, teaching foreign languages is also crucial. Not only does it help promote intercultural exchange and goodwill among different nations, strong foreign language skills among civil servants can also improve a state's ability to gather foreign intelligence.

In foreign policy, education has become a significant concern with regard to the global war on terrorism. Children and youth who become indoctrinated with ideologies and hostile messages against others can more easily be convinced to take up violence in the name of their cause when they become young adults.

By contrast, education in the liberal arts can counteract these tendencies as it teaches young people critical thinking skills, that is, it teaches them *how* to think. Schools that teach children only *what* to think rather than *how* to think will produce adults who have never learned to debate and challenge authority. As Gerstein comments: "On the surface, this does not appear to be a major issue, until one understands that a lack of debate in the educational process can translate into an inability to engage in meaningful dialogues later with respect to other issues such as democratic institutions, rights of women, and religious tolerance."[541] In other words, an education system that fosters critical thinking skills and the art of debate can make liberal democracies possible and durable. And the establishment of thriving democracies around the world will have global security implications, as democracies purportedly do not go to war against each other.[542]

Providing better educational opportunities for young people in developing countries also helps to foster economic development and enables young people to choose between a variety of jobs and hence become productive members of society. As is noted above, high birth rates are a challenge in many developing countries. As Gerstein explains, these demographic trends "will result in large youthful populations that must be given something productive and fulfilling to occupy their energies, or the result will be large disenfranchised, unemployable populations that will likely lead to instability and conflict".[543] Through education, these energies can be channelled towards productive ends. Particularly important will be the inclusion of the "liberal arts and the study of comparative religions" in the school curriculum,[544] which helps to raise young people's awareness of diversity and their appreciation of tolerance.

States today have an increased interest as part of their national security strategy in stabilising and possibly democratising states that have experienced instability and internal armed conflict. States that expect to be contributing to post-conflict reconstruction and state building projects should have educational experts involved in helping to build a good education system in post-conflict societies, which will serve as a foundation for social peace and economic development in the fledgling state.

The Division on Education, Intellectual Excellence, Culture and the Arts can allow itself to be guided by the eight education policy recommendations developed in a previous work on *The Role of Education in Global Security*. It is sufficient here to recapitulate them briefly:

1) *Empowerment and Development*: Any education system should teach students critical thinking skills from early on and empower them to become mature, independent-thinking citizens.
2) *Global Knowledge of Histories and Cultures*: Education systems should teach prospective leaders in the private and public sectors of wealthy countries about the growing economic gap between countries and among citizens, and the many ways poverty and inequality can trigger violence. This knowledge can motivate leaders of wealthy states and institutions to help meet the Millennium Development Goals.
3) *Cultural Respect and Understanding*: Schools should play their part in teaching students tolerance and the peaceful resolution of conflicts.
4) *Communication, Exchange and Exposure*: Schools everywhere in the world should support foreign language instruction and participate in international student exchanges and communication.
5) *Global Citizenry Through Responsible Media and Responsible Political Statements*: Providing people with access to a breadth of information sources will make them less susceptible to one-sided information.
6) *Global Values and Equality*: Educational institutions should promote universal values of tolerance and respect for human rights.
7) *Abuse of Knowledge*: Citizens need to be educated about the ways information can be manipulated and how they can pro-

tect themselves from falling prey to propaganda and indoctrination.

8) *Other Truths and Views*: Schools need to foster cultural awareness and convey to students in a non-judgmental fashion the different ways that the world's multiple cultures and religions try to make sense of the world. [545]

Promoting these eight recommendations in educational institutions at home as well as encouraging and supporting other states to do the same can make an enormous contribution to long-lasting peace and stability in the world.

3. Division on Future Trajectories and Contingencies

This division addresses long-term security threats and potential new threats that might emerge. There are at least four future scenarios that this division might consider based on current global trends. One trend could be a shifting balance in economic power, with India and China starting to play a more weighty role in the global economy and ultimately to gain more political clout as well.[546] The challenge of this scenario is for Western states to adapt to a globalised world that is no longer as strongly dominated by Western values but includes and embraces Asian and other cultural values and practices as well.

A second scenario, which the US-based National Intelligence Council (NIC) refers to as "pax Americana", is one that presumes that US global dominance will consolidate itself in the coming decades.[547] For the United States, this would mean that it needs to win world public opinion to its side and prevent hostile anti-US alliances from forming by convincing other states that the United States would not use its power to harm other states and operates within the limits of international norms. For other states, it would mean that maintaining a good relationship with the United States were crucial for their own national security. Furthermore, close relations with the United States might also enable other states to influence US policy and convince it to pursue goals that serve the long-term security interests of the international community.

A third scenario might be the emergence of a global movement based on a dangerous radical ideology.[548] States can take preventive measures by providing a domestic context that ensures the well-being of all citizens through good governance, adequate health and social services, and a good economic infrastructure, and by helping other states to achieve the same. Only by reassuring people around the world that they can look forward to a better future by embracing democracy, respect for human rights and capitalism will they reject ideologies that oppose the latter. A fourth scenario that the National Intelligence Council identifies is one whereby international concerns about WMD proliferation lead to intrusive security measures around the world. These measures might succeed in curtailing the trade in WMD, but at great cost. The "real victim", according to the NIC, may be globalisation.[549] Therefore, contingency planning for this scenario would involve the development of counterproliferation strategies that are less disruptive of the globalisation process, along with the attempt to convince the NSC to make WMD proliferation a priority national security concern to avoid this fourth scenario altogether.

Of course, these are only a few scenarios for future threats that this NSC division might consider. Other issues, for example, might include contingency planning for the possible disastrous consequences of global warming; shortages in global energy supply; and the eruptions of new internal wars in states at risk of failure.

4. Division on Conflict Analysis and Prevention

Unfortunately, it is to be expected that intra-state conflicts will continue to plague the international security environment for the foreseeable future. The consequences of such conflicts could be state failure or collapse, mass killings, environmental destruction and refugee flows, to name just a few. Every national security council should therefore have people on staff who are preoccupied with studying these types of conflicts and devising possible preventive measures. It is a fairly new field for states to study but highly relevant in an interconnected world, where domestic developments have security implications for other states. As a model, the division may adopt the Conflict Analysis Framework (CAF) developed by the World Bank. The CAF identifies and studies six key factors that influence conflict: "social and ethnic relations; governance and political institutions; human rights and security; economic structure and performance; environment and natural resources; and external factors".[550] The Division on Conflict Analysis and Prevention is concerned with the long-term. It would study the causes of past and present conflicts and observe developments in all five security dimensions to spot future conflict trends and potential hot spots.

5. Division on Good Governance

This is a watchdog division that seeks to prevent national security policy from becoming unduly "hijacked" or monopolised by a single interest group within the country. It makes recommendations for laws to improve government transparency and to fight corruption. The division's role in the NSC is to ensure that security threats and policy interests are identified through as objective a procedure as possible. It continually reminds policy makers that the welfare of the common citizen always comes before the interests of the few.

In any free democracy, political parties, lobby and interest groups, think tanks and the media will continue to voice their opinions and try to influence policy making. The Division on Good Governance attempts to ensure that the NSC considers the concerns of the different interest groups in the context of the overall security and economic interests of the country. It may also suggest laws to help to maintain diversity in the media, so that the public dialogue on security policy remains free and balanced.

Moreover, the division would oversee the hiring process at the NSC and related government agencies and departments to ensure that the staff is selected on a purely meritocratic basis, in accordance with non-discriminatory rules of government hiring. National security is too important an issue to be left to people who lack the proper qualifications. Maintaining meritocratic standards also helps to prevent one single group within a country dominating the government due to privileged family ties or financial status. Finally, and most importantly, maintaining fair and transparent competition for employment in the government helps to ensure government legitimacy and hence domestic stability.

6. Division on the Rights of Women, Children, Minorities and the Economically Disadvantaged

As the UN Fourth World Conference on Women stated at its outset: "Human rights and fundamental freedoms are the birthright of all human beings; their protection and promotion is the first responsibility of Governments".[551] Hence, a national security council needs to have people on staff whose task it is to ensure that this goal becomes an integral component of national security policy. Together with the home department, this division recommends ways to ensure that international human rights norms, and especially the rights of women, children and minorities, are observed at home, both with regard to nationals and citizens of other countries. This includes, among other things, laws against child pornography and domestic violence, and equal opportunities legislation.

The division is tasked with ensuring that any state action pursued in the name of national security observes and helps promote universal human rights norms. For instance, if a country decided to send troops abroad to participate in a peacebuilding or state building mission, this NSC division can suggest ways to make sure that the rights of women and children are observed and promoted during the mission. Hence, the troops would need to receive extra training to become sensitised to specific women's and children's issues. As women in poor countries are often harder hit by illiteracy than men, peacebuilding troops, for example, may have to make sure to spread important information via easily understandable brochures.[552] Governments that try to strengthen democracy in another country by helping to build a strong civil society may want to ensure that they also support emerging women's organisations. Furthermore, governments that help a peacebuilding effort by sponsoring schools would have to insist that boys and girls are given equal access to educational institutions.

Similarly, the division would ensure that the rights of minorities, as well as of the economically disadvantaged, inside and outside the country, were protected when action was taken in the name of national security. This is in both the moral interest and the pragmatic self-interest of every state, because discrimination against specific groups of people can lead to violence. The division can serve as a constant reminder to national security policy makers that no lasting peace at home and abroad can be achieved without empowering those groups that have traditionally been the weakest and most vulnerable members of society.

7. Division on Lessons Learned, History and Doctrines

This division employs historians to evaluate past policies pursued by the state and other states to assess the advantages and disadvantages of a particular policy or doctrine. The division would advise policy makers and educate them about past mistakes made by states that found themselves in a similar situation. As decision researcher Craig Kirkwood explains, "people tend to focus too much on what happened in the immediate past" while neglecting "other possibilities that may be more likely" but have happened in the more distant past.[553]

The division also assists policy makers to distinguish between what they know and what they think they know, between an event that policy makers have been confronted with in the past and an event that nobody has been confronted with before. Decision researcher Daniel Brooks explains that humans tend to be not very good at judging their ability to handle problems that have not been solved before:

> Research over the past half-decade has shown that as situations become more complex, people feel more confidence in their opinions about how those situations should be addressed....Ask someone how best to fix your refrigerator and they may be hesitant to help – they have little confidence in their ability to fix appliances because they may have tried this in the past and know that they can fail. Ask the same person how best to handle the withdrawal from Iraq or stabilize global oil supplies and they may have very specific recommendations that they are willing to argue for passionately. The reason is that there is little experience trying out one's ideas as sovereign manager of the Middle East or global energy – and, as a result, little experience with failure there. The result is that as complexity increases, direct experience is less common and personal confidence goes up, not down, on what the best path forward is.[554]

This division can thus alert members of the national security council not to become stuck in a struggle between competing "expert" advice but to recognise the complexity of the problem, dissect it and learn from the new situation while adjusting the response according to the new lessons learned while solving it.

8. Division for Upholding Values of Morality, Justice and Dignity in Policy Decisions

This division seeks to ensure that basic moral values are observed when making security policy. Basic moral values are stressed here because the attempt to adjust political practice to any elaborate moral theory is an almost impossible, even self-defeating, task for any state. As political philosopher Michael Walzer puts it, states "operate in a world of conflicting interest and values where they are constantly forced into compromises which are, as we say, morally compromising".[555] But both those who argue against the application of any moral principles to foreign policy making and those who argue for the rigid pursuit of a moral agenda regardless of pragmatic political circumstances are mistaken. Instead, a moral foreign policy involves the observance of basic moral principles regarding the responsibilities of the state towards its citizens and towards fellow human beings across the world. This also entails respect for basic just war principles, which limit the use of force by states to legitimate self-defence, collective self-defence, the use of force sanctioned by the UN Security Council and to rescue people threatened by genocide.

Walzer's "four propositions for a more moral foreign policy" sums up the moral obligations of a state rather well and thus provides a useful framework for national security councils around the world to adopt as a guiding principle:

> The first obligation of…any state is its Hobbesian obligation to protect the life and liberty of its own citizens. The second obligation is not to inflict harm on the citizens of other states. The third obligation is to help citizens of other states, when it's possible to do that, avoid or escape crimes and disasters of collective life, genocide, tyranny, conquest, ethnic cleansing, famine and disease. The fourth obligation is to help the citizens of other states, when they want to be helped, to build decent and non-repressive political systems.[556]

As Walzer explains, these principles are general enough so that they can be applied by states with various cultural and religious backgrounds,[557] as well as by states that strictly separate religion and state affairs.

Observing moral values in foreign policy means that states should not infringe on the dignity and sovereignty of other states, even if other states sometimes disagree or promote values we do not necessarily approve of (as long as these values do not violate universal human norms). States can thus allow themselves to be guided by a "global good neighbour ethic". As scholars of the US-based International Relations Center put it, "Good neighbors do not dictate to others how to live their lives. Instead, they respect differences and diversity in their neighborhoods."[558] Observing basic moral values and just war principles contributes to the long-term national security of states. The division thus ensures that the government does not take any rash decisions to protect its short-term security interests but takes actions that will be viewed as legitimate and rightful by a majority of civilised nations at any time.

In sum, an ideal NSC provides the leadership of a state with security-related information and suggests policy options in any given situation. The different groups and divisions of the proposed council enable the NSC Board to examine security problems in a broad context – both horizontally and historically. On the one hand, the broad range of topics covered by the NSC staff ensures that policy makers are aware of the different security dimensions and understand how different and apparently separate issues interrelate. On the other hand, the security council staff can put current issues in their historical context by showing how similar situations have been handled in the past, and project the problem into the future by suggesting how the problem should be handled so as not to make the situation worse in the future. The inclusion of Principles and Future Trajectories Divisions in a modern NSC helps security policy makers to align their policies with universal values of human rights and dignity, to promote good governance and justice at home and abroad, and to allocate resources for conflict prevention and long-term strategic planning. The proposed NSC model is based on the notion that lasting peace and security can only be achieved if states focus on the multi-dimensionality of today's security environment, form mutually beneficial security relationships with other states in every dimension of security, and boost human creativity through fruitful exchanges and interactions with other cultural and civilizational entities.

4. A Proposed NSC Decision-making Process

Having explored the different types of issues and concerns that an ideal national security council in the 21st century would be dealing with, it remains to explain how such a council would function in practice. This section demonstrates the security policy-making process in a general model, which may be adjusted to fit different systems of government.

It is important that there is enough room in the formal policy development process to allow for informal meetings and exchanges. At the same time, the process must be structured to allow policy options to be put forward efficiently while leaving no important group or input out of the process. Moreover, as a study of the NSC process in the United States found, "formal processes are also especially valuable when introducing new factors into the traditional national security equation (e.g., economics) and as a road map for new process players".[559]

(a) The Six-step Process

Figure 4 presents a model for a six-step security policy-making process. The process is formulated in very general and broad terms, and each government would need to adjust and refine it in accordance with its governing structure and constitution.

1. The politically responsible authority of a state (president, prime minister, elected government) tasks the NSC to study a security-related issue. The NSC board then assigns main responsibility for the issue to one or sometimes two Issue Groups. Any of the Principles and Future Trajectories Divisions can take up and study the issue as well

Figure 4: NSC Security Policy Process in the Three Pillar Model

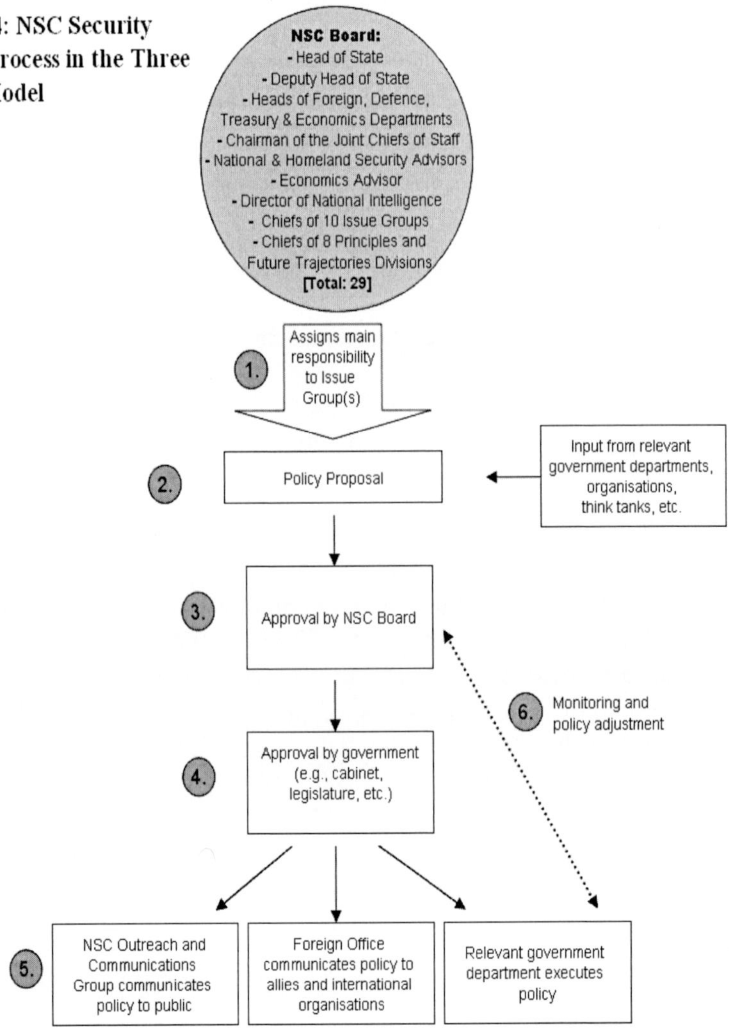

and bring up any relevant concerns to the NSC and the Issue Group that has been assigned to work on the problem.

2. The Issue Group with assigned main responsibility then draws up a policy proposal that includes a choice of options for the government to tackle the security issue.

3. The policy proposal is then circulated among all members of the NSC Board. The Board discusses the proposal and includes the inputs and recommendations from the Board members, as well as other relevant inputs coming from think tanks and academics in the country.

4. The revised policy proposal is then passed on to the leader of the state who, if he or she decides to implement one of the proposed policy options, follows all the necessary steps for policy implementation prescribed by the country's constitution, which might mean that the proposal would need to go through the cabinet or the legislature for final approval.

5. The policy is then assigned to the relevant government department for execution. Moreover, the Outreach and Communication Group is tasked with devising and implementing a public communications strategy for the policy. The Issue Group that has worked out the policy proposal thereby stays in close contact with the Outreach and Communication Group to ensure that the group has all the relevant background information on the security issue and understands the rationale for the government's policy to combat the security threat. Finally, the Foreign Office of the state is tasked with communicating the policy to relevant allies and international organisations.

6. While the policy is being executed, the NSC Board and the Issue Group that has worked out the policy proposal closely monitor the policy's implementation. It assists the executing department to adjust the policy to newly arising and unexpected circumstances. The NSC Board will also need to monitor the constant information age dialectic between the government's execution of the policy and the reaction of the public through the media and decide whether it is appropriate to give in to public opposition and adjust the policy accordingly, or simply to improve the communication strategy.

Box 1: 13 Characteristics of the Proposed NSC from A to M

1. *Autonomous*: The NSC makes policy proposals that are free of departmental or political biases.
2. *Broadly based*: The breadth of topics covered by different Issue Groups and Principles and Future Trajectories Divisions does justice to the fact that no area of 21st century policy making remains untouched by security-related issues.
3. *Communication-savvy*: The NSC recognises that good communication with the public at home and abroad is an indispensable aspect of a sustainable security policy.
4. *Decision-oriented*: The NSC has a slim decision-making structure, acknowledging the fact that the window for making decisive policy decisions can be very narrow in today's instant and interdependent world.
5. *Ethical*: The NSC acknowledges that acting in accordance with universal ethical values is necessary not just because it is the right thing to do, but because it shapes the image of the state in an age where every policy move is closely scrutinised by the media and personal blogs. Ethically grounded policy will help to ensure the long-term survival of the state.
6. *Flexible*: The drafting process for NSC policy proposals allows enough room for informal exchanges among members of the different NSC divisions and thus ensures that every NSC member who could potentially contribute to the policy formulation process can do so. During policy implementation, the NSC is quick to adjust its security policy proposals to changing international circumstances.
7. *Global*: The NSC looks at security-related challenges abroad from a global perspective by taking into account that insecurity in one part of the world can have security implications in the most unexpected places. It understands the process of globalisation and the interconnected nature of the global system.
8. *Humane*: The NSC places enhanced importance on promoting the overall well-being of humans around the world. It stresses the need for human security at home and abroad and makes the fight against disease, poverty and all forms of oppression a central part of its security policy.

Box 1 *continued*

9. *Innovative*: The NSC understands the security-related importance of keeping up with technological innovations. It supports technological progress at home to remain one step ahead of the country's enemies when it comes to neutralising technologically based threats.
10. *Just*: The NSC makes the promotion of justice a central aspect of all its policy proposals. It understands that without global justice there can never be international stability and peace.
11. *Knowledgeable*: The NSC employs experts from a range of different fields and draws on the knowledge of the best and the brightest in the country. Moreover, the NSC disposes of a wealth of first-rate intelligence collected from various intelligence sources and carefully put together by intelligence experts within the council. The NSC also employs historians able to relate their rich knowledge of lessons learned from the past to NSC members so that NSC proposals are made based on all available information relevant to the particular security issue.
12. *Long-term oriented*: The NSC is not tied down by the urgent security issues of the moment. It has people on staff whose task it is to evaluate the long-term security implications of proposed government policies and spot potential future security threats that might be tackled before they become urgent issues.
13. *Multicultural*: The NSC takes into account the multicultural nature of global society in the 21st century. It has cultural experts on staff who ensure that a country's security policy towards other states respects the cultural values of the people implicated by the policy. It contributes to enhanced cultural understanding and cooperation and works towards the long-term goal of achieving transcivilizational synergy.

5. Towards a Sustainable National Security Doctrine

The proposed NSC schema developed in this chapter lays out the different aspects and facets of 21st century security policy that need to be taken into account in devising a security strategy that is sustainable in the long term. Depending on the size and resources of a country, the number of NSC staff may vary greatly. It is important that a national security council, no matter what its size, considers in some form or another many of the issues identified in this chapter when making security policy.

The proposed NSC takes the new global circumstances of today's instant and interdependent world into account. It is based on the three pillars summarised in chapter 4: 1) *multi-sum security,*[560] the notion that security needs to be based on justice, multilateralism and multidimensionality (including human, environmental, national, transnational and transcultural security); 2) *symbiotic realism*,[561] the idea that in an interdependent world, states can form security relationships that are mutually beneficial; and 3) *transcivilizational synergy*,[562] the necessity for the world's diverse cultures and civilizations to create synergetic relationships as a vital building block for international peace and security. Sustainable national security in a transnational world needs to rest on these three pillars. This security principle is illustrated in Figure 5.

Apart from the traditional components of defence and homeland security, a national security council today needs to include appropriate policy groups dealing with aspects of our instant and interdependent world. The inclusion of Principles and Future Trajectories Divisions in a modern NSC reflects the need for security policy makers to align their policies with universal values of human rights and dignity, to promote good governance and justice at home and abroad, and to allocate resources for conflict prevention and long-term strategic planning. Only by taking into account the multiplicity of actors and several different security dimensions, as well as the need for multilateral cooperation and transcivilizational synergy, can a national security strategy be sustainable in the 21st century.

Figure 5: The Three Pillars of *Sustainable National Security* in a Transnational World

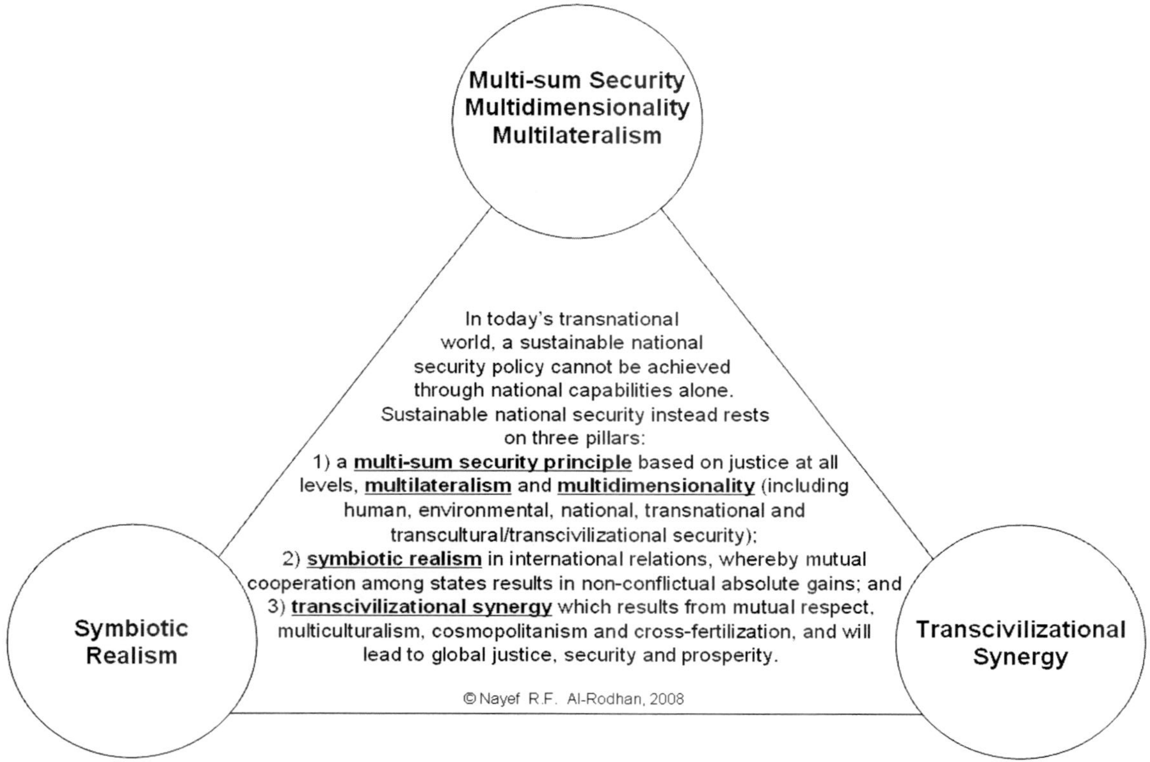

CHAPTER 7

CONCLUSIONS

The concept of national security has evolved along with the changing international security environment. States today face a broad variety of security issues. Unlike the past three centuries, the threat of foreign invasion no longer figures at the top of most states' security concerns. This traditional threat has given way to a plethora of so-called non-traditional threats that currently preoccupy states. Unlike the former, the latter rarely put the territorial integrity of states in jeopardy. Rather, these are threats that endanger the lives, livelihood or well-being of a state's population. Chapter 4 has identified eleven different areas from which security threats to states emanate today. These range from computer viruses to clashes between civilizations; from a global economic recession to the uncontrollable spread of an infectious disease; and from mass migration to global warming.

States have adapted their national security strategies or doctrines accordingly. As the historical discussion in chapter 2 has demonstrated, states have regularly updated their national security doctrines according to changed international circumstances. Almost everywhere in the world, the definition of national security broadened after the Cold War, and the growing interconnectedness of human activity and state action is increasingly being factored into the security equation. Particularly striking in the latest security doctrines of the European Union and the United States is the notion that the physical and material security of human beings everywhere in the world are a prerequisite for creating increased international peace and stability, which in turn is a precondition for the lasting national security of every individual state. This partly reflects the realisation that poverty and oppression around the world are an important cause of violence and many other transnational threats.

The information age has shaped the national security policies of states. Every state action today is under close scrutiny by the global media, and policy makers, more than ever before, need to take public opinion at home and abroad into account when acting in the name of national security. Developing a good communication strategy and avoiding the violation of international norms, human rights and humanitarian law have become increasingly important features of successful national security policy making.

Yet, the national security structures of states have only evolved slowly. They tend to change much more slowly than the security environment in which they operate. The frequently heard criticism that militaries tend to prepare for the last war may also apply to civilian national security structures. Changes to the national security apparatuses within states are often merely cosmetic, reflecting ad hoc responses to a sudden security breach rather than a fundamental rethinking of the state's approach to national security in the light of new threats and international priorities. As is discussed in chapter 3, more and more states are starting to create a unified institutionalised setting within the government to deal with security-related issues. In these national security councils, experts and members of the government executive can meet, identify the state's security priorities and coordinate the state's national security policy.

This book argues that a national security council structure that is embedded in the executive branch of governments is the right solution to effectively address threats to national security in the 21st century. However, an ideal NSC structure would need to be significantly broader than existing ones around the world. An NSC today must include staff that deal with a broad range of security issues and dimensions, as well as with long-term threat prevention and the maintenance of ethical standards in the conduct of security policy.

To make national security policy sustainable, it needs to be based on three pillars. These are multi-sum security, symbiotic realism and transcivilizational synergy. This means that sustainable peace and security can only be achieved if states focus on the multi-dimensionality of today's security environment, form mutually beneficial security relationships with other states in every security dimension, and enrich their own culture and boost human creativity through fruitful exchanges and interactions with other cultures and civilizations.

References

[1] M. Anderson and J. Apap, "Changing Conceptions of Security and their Implications for EU Justice and Home Affairs Cooperation," Centre for European Policy Studies (CEPS) Policy Brief No. 26, October 2002, http://www.ceps.be, p. 2.
[2] D.M. Snow, *National Security for a New Era: Globalization and Geopolitics* (Second Edition) (New York: Pearson Education, Inc., 2007), p. 381.
[3] A. Wolfers, *Discord and Collaboration: Essays on International Politics* (Baltimore: Johns Hopkins University Press, 1962), p. 150.
[4] "National Security Policy," Geneva Centre for the Democratic Control of Armed Forces (DCAF) Backgrounder, November 2005, www.dcaf.ch/publications/backgrounders, p. 1.
[5] *Ibid.*
[6] G. Allison, "National and International Security," in J.S. Nye Jr. and J.D. Donahue (eds.), *Governance in a Globalizing World* (Washington, DC: Brookings Institution Press, 2000), p. 76.
[7] Anderson and Apap, *op. cit.*, note 1.
[8] *Ibid.*
[9] "Democratic Peace Bibliography," accessed on 6 August 2007, http://www.hawaii.edu/powerkills/BIBLIO.HTML.
[10] V. Ferraro, "Globalizing Weakness: Is Global Poverty a Threat to the Interests of States?" Environmental Change and Security Program (ECSP) Report, Issue 9, 2003, http://www.wilsoncenter.org/index.cfm?topic_id=1413&fuseaction=topics.publications&group_id=43158, p. 14.
[11] *Ibid.*
[12] R.B. Persaud, "An Alternative Way of Thinking through Security Relations," accessed on 26 April 2007, http://www.koreagsis.ac.kr/research/journal/vol6/6-04-Randolph%20B.%20Persaud.pdf, p. 1.
[13] R. Ullman, "Redefining Security," *International Security* Vol. 8, No. 1, 1983, p. 33.
[14] The Commission on America's National Interests, *America's National Interests* (Cambridge, Massachusetts: Belfer Center for Science and International Affairs, 2000), http://www.nixoncenter.org/publications/monographs/nationalinterests.pdf, p. 15.
[15] Allison, *op. cit.*, note 6, p. 76.
[16] S.A. Cambone, *A New Structure for National Security Policy Planning* (Washington, DC: Center for Strategic and International Studies, 1998), pp. 8-9.
[17] *Ibid.,* pp. 9-10.
[18] *Ibid.,* pp. 12-13.
[19] *Ibid.,* p. 13.
[20] P.J. Garrity, "Interests and Issues: Perspectives on Future Challenges to US Security," in S.A. Cambone, *op. cit.*, note 16, p. 128.
[21] Cambone, *op. cit.*, note 16, p. 19.
[22] *Encarta Encyclopedia,* accessed on 5 August 2007, http://encarta.msn.com/encyclopedia_761569621/Great_Wall_(China).html, s.v. "Great Wall (China)."
[23] H.A. Kissinger, *Diplomacy* (New York: Simon & Schuster, 1994), p. 61.
[24] B. Russett, H. Starr and D. Kinsella, *World Politics: The Menu for Choice* (7th Edition) (Belmont, CA: Wadsworth/Thomson Learning, 2004), p. 54.

[25] J. Elliott, "War and Peace in Europe, 1618-1648," in K. Bussmann and H. Schilling (eds.), *1648: War and Peace in Europe* (Osnabrueck, Germany: Muenster, 1999), p. 39.
[26] Persaud, *op. cit.*, note 12, p. 6.
[27] A. Moseley, "Political Realism," The Internet Encyclopedia of Philosophy, 2006, http://www.iep.utm.edu/p/polreal.htm.
[28] Thucydides, *The Peloponnesian War* (New York: E. P. Dutton, 1910), Section 5.89.
[29] *Stanford Encyclopedia of Philosophy*, 13 September 2005, http://plato.stanford.edu/entries/machiavelli/#2, s.v. "Niccolo Machiavelli."
[30] M. Corks, "Hobbesian Egoism in Contemporary Realism," 7 April 2000, http://theorem.ca/~mvcorks/code/pacs316.html.
[31] T. Hobbes, *Leviathan,* C.B. MacPherson (ed.) (Aylesbury: Hazell, Watson and Viney Ltd., 1651:1972), p. 161.
[32] Corks, *op. cit.,* note 30.
[33] Kissinger, *op. cit.,* note 23, p. 58.
[34] *Ibid.,* p. 61.
[35] *Ibid.,* p. 74.
[36] *Ibid.,* p. 96.
[37] W. Levi, "Ideology, Interests, and Foreign Policy," *International Studies Quarterly*, Vol. 14, No. 1, March 1970, p. 9.
[38] Kissinger, *op. cit.,* note 23, pp. 95-96.
[39] *Ibid.,* p. 96.
[40] *Encyclopedia Britannica Online*, accessed on 16 November 2007, http://www.britannica.com/eb/article-9040842/Holy-Alliance, s.v. "Holy Alliance."
[41] Kissinger, *op. cit.,* note 23, p. 79.
[42] *Ibid.,* pp. 121-122.
[43] *Ibid.,* p. 104.
[44] *Ibid.,* p. 137.
[45] *Ibid.,* p. 128.
[46] *Ibid.,* pp. 168-169.
[47] F.J. Gavin, "To End All Wars: Woodrow Wilson and the Quest for a New World Order," *Orbis,* Fall 1997, BNET Research Center, http://findarticles.com/p/articles/mi_m0365/is_n4_v41/ai_20377527.
[48] Kissinger, *op. cit.,* note 23, p. 247.
[49] *Ibid.*
[50] *Ibid.,* p. 248.
[51] "President Woodrow Wilson's Fourteen Points," accessed on 6 June 2007, http://net.lib.byu.edu/~rdh7/wwi/1918/14points.html.
[52] Kissinger, *op. cit.,* note 23, pp. 244-245.
[53] "Activities of the European Union: Summaries of Legislation," European Union, accessed on 23 July 2007, http://europa.eu/scadplus/treaties/maastricht_en.htm#EUROPEANUNION.
[54] "A Secure Europe in a Better World: European Security Strategy," The European Institute for Security Studies, 12 December 2003, http://www.iss-eu.org/solana/solanae.pdf, p. 7.
[55] *Ibid.,* p. 9.
[56] *Ibid.*
[57] *Ibid.,* p. 10.
[58] *Ibid.,* p. 7.

[59] *Ibid.*, p. 8.
[60] T. Luhde and P. Schmidt, "Formulierung europäischer Sicherheitsinteressen für ein strategisch handelndes Europa," *Beitraege zur Sicherheitspolitik*, Bundesministerium für Landesverteidigung Wien, February 2007.
[61] *Ibid.*, pp. 39-40.
[62] "Russia," Library of Congress Country Studies," accessed on 24 July 2007, http://lcweb2.loc.gov/cgi-bin/query/r?frd/cstdy:@field(DOCID+ru0181).
[63] *Ibid.*
[64] "Russian/Soviet Doctrine," Globalsecurity.org, accessed on 13 August 2007, http://www.globalsecurity.org/wmd/world/russia/intro.htm.
[65] "Russia," *op. cit.*, note 62.
[66] "Russian/Soviet Doctrine," *op. cit.*, note 64.
[67] C.A. Wallander, "Russian National Security Policy in 2000," PONARS Policy Memo 102, Harvard University, January 2000, p. 1.
[68] "The National Security Concept of the Russian Federation," accessed on 24 July 2007, http://www.ciaonet.org/wps/sea03/.
[69] *Ibid.*
[70] *Ibid.*
[71] *Ibid.*
[72] *Ibid.*
[73] "Russian/Soviet Doctrine," *op. cit.*, note 64.
[74] Wallander, *op. cit.*, note 67, p. 4.
[75] *Ibid.*, p. 5.
[76] *Ibid.*
[77] *Ibid.*
[78] F.P. Sempa, "US National Security Doctrines Historically Viewed: A Commentary," AmericanDiplomacy.org, accessed on 15 May 2007, http://www.unc.edu/depts/diplomat/archives_roll/2004_04-06/sempa_nsd/sempa_nsd.html.
[79] "Washington's Farewell Address 1796," The Avalon Project, Yale Law School, accessed on 6 June 2007, http://www.yale.edu/lawweb/avalon/washing.htm.
[80] *Ibid.*
[81] *Ibid.*
[82] *Ibid.*
[83] Sempa, *op. cit.*, note 78.
[84] "The Monroe Doctrine (1823)," International Information Programs, US Department of State, accessed on 6 June 2007, http://usinfo.state.gov/usa/infousa/facts/democrac/50.htm.
[85] *Ibid.*
[86] *Ibid.*
[87] Sempa, *op. cit.*, note 78.
[88] "John L. O'Sullivan on *Manifest Destiny*, 1839," accessed on 6 June 2007, http://www.mtholyoke.edu/acad/intrel/osulliva.htm.
[89] "Alfred Thayer Mahan," U-S-history.com, accessed on 6 June 2007, http://www.u-s-history.com/pages/h811.html.
[90] Sempa, *op. cit.*, note 78.
[91] *Ibid.*
[92] *Ibid.*
[93] *Ibid.*
[94] *Ibid.*

[95] *Ibid.*
[96] *Ibid.*
[97] *Ibid.*
[98] G.F. Kennan, "The Sources of Soviet Conduct," The History Guide, accessed on 7 June 2007, http://www.historyguide.org/europe/kennan.html.
[99] "President Harry S. Truman's Address Before A Joint Session Of Congress, March 12, 1947," The Avalon Project at Yale Law School, accessed on 7 June 2007, http://www.yale.edu/lawweb/avalon/trudoc.htm.
[100] "NSC 68: United States Objectives and Programs for National Security," Federation of American Scientists website, accessed on 7 June 2007, http://www.fas.org/irp/offdocs/nsc-hst/nsc-68.htm.
[101] Sempa, *op. cit.*, note 78.
[102] "Mutual Assured Destruction," Nuclear Files: Key Issues, accessed on 7 June 2007, http://www.nuclearfiles.org/menu/key-issues/nuclear-weapons/history/cold-war/strategy/strategy-mutual-assured-destruction.htm.
[103] Persaud, *op. cit.*, note 12, pp. 7-8.
[104] H. Morgenthau and K. Thompson, *Politics Among Nations* (6th edition) (New York: McGraw-Hill, 1985), p. 165.
[105] G.F. Kennan, *American Diplomacy 1900-1950* (Chicago: University of Chicago Press, 1951), pp. 101-102.
[106] Kissinger, *op. cit.,* note 23, p. 742.
[107] Sempa, *op. cit.*, note 78.
[108] J.P. Harahan, "INF Treaty Process," in *On-Site Inspections Under the INF Treaty: A History of the On-Site Inspection Agency and Treaty Implementation, 1988-1991,* Federation of American Scientists, 1993, http://www.fas.org/nuke/control/inf/infbook/ch3.html.
[109] S. Zhang and M. Jacobs, "The Soviet Invasion of Afghanistan 1979-1989," December 2001, http://nhs.needham.k12.ma.us/cur/Baker_00/2002-p4/baker_p4_12-01_mj_sz/#back.
[110] "Reagan Doctrine, 1985," US Department of State, accessed on 7 June 2007, http://www.state.gov/r/pa/ho/time/rd/17741.htm.
[111] Sempa, *op. cit.*, note 78.
[112] *Ibid.*
[113] Close Up Foundation, *Current Issues: Critical Policy Choices Facing the Nation and the World* (Alexandria, VA: Close Up Foundation, 2004), p. 196.
[114] Sempa, *op. cit.*, note 78.
[115] *Ibid.*
[116] "The National Security Strategy of the United States," The White House, President George W. Bush, September 2002, http://www.whitehouse.gov/nsc/nss.pdf.
[117] M.E. O'Hanlon, S.E. Rice and J.B. Steinberg, "The New National Security Strategy and Preemption," Policy Brief 113, The Brookings Institution, http://www.brook.edu/comm/policybriefs/pb113.htm.
[118] "The National Security Strategy of the United States," *op. cit.*, note 116.
[119] *Ibid.*
[120] "The National Security Strategy of the United States," The White House, President George W. Bush, March 2006, http://www.whitehouse.gov/nsc/nss/2006/.
[121] *Ibid.*

[122] Ch.W. Hughes, "A Multidimensional Approach to Security: The Case of Japan," Ridgway Center for International Security Studies, University of Pittsburgh, 2006, http://www.ridgway.pitt.edu/docs/working_papers/PENE/HughesFinalCopy.pdf.
[123] *Ibid.*, p. 6.
[124] *Ibid.*
[125] B. Singh, "Japan's Post-Cold War Security Policy: Bringing Back the Normal State," *Contemporary Southeast Asia,* Vol. 24, No. 1, 2002, http://www.questia.com/googleScholar.qst;jsessionid=Gymfhq2V2JQQRnhZV65mLgyNG0DyNp8rMQMXZmtW8K1LCB1cznWy!-1234854660?docId=5002471220.
[126] Hughes, *op. cit*, note 122, p. 6.
[127] Singh, *op. cit*, note 125.
[128] *Ibid.*
[129] *Ibid.*
[130] *Ibid.*
[131] Hughes, *op. cit.*, note 122, p. 8.
[132] *Ibid.*
[133] *Ibid.*
[134] *Ibid.*, p. 9.
[135] Singh, *op. cit*, note 125.
[136] *Ibid.*
[137] *Ibid.*
[138] *Ibid.*
[139] *Ibid.*
[140] *Ibid.*
[141] *Ibid.*
[142] Hughes, *op. cit.*, note 122, p. 10.
[143] *Ibid.*
[144] M.D. Swaine and A.J. Tellis, "Interpreting China's Grand Strategy," RAND Research Brief *Interpreting China's Grand Strategy: Past, Present and Future,* 2000, http://www.rand.org/pubs/research_briefs/RB61/index1.html.
[145] *Ibid.*
[146] *Ibid.*
[147] *Ibid.*
[148] *Ibid.*
[149] Lt Col. K.B. Wooton, "Chinese National Security Strategy: Implications for a 21st Century Air Force," a Research Report Submitted to Air Force Fellows, CADRE/AR, April 2005, p. 12.
[150] *Ibid.*
[151] *Ibid.,* p. 11.
[152] *Ibid.*, p. 17.
[153] *Ibid.,* p. 11.
[154] T. Akihiko, "The Rise of China and Changes in the Balance of Power in East Asia," accessed on 17 July 2007, http://www.jfir.or.jp/e/research_e/seminar2/conver_3.htm.
[155] "PRC: 2004 White Paper on National Defense Published," White Paper on China's National Defense in 2004, Federation of American Scientists, 2004, http://www.fas.org/nuke/guide/china/doctrine/natdef2004.html; "China's National Defense in 2006," Information Office of the State Council of the People's Republic of China, December 2006, http://www.china.org.cn/english/features/book/194421.htm.

[156] Akihiko, *op. cit.*, note 154.
[157] A.I. Johnston, "Realism and Chinese Security Policy in the Post-Cold War Period," in E.B. Kapstein and M. Mastanduno (eds.), *Unipolar Politics: Realism and State Strategies After the Cold War,* http://www.ciaonet.org.library3.webster.edu/book/kapstein/kapstein08.html.
[158] *Ibid.*
[159] *Ibid.*
[160] *Ibid.*
[161] *Ibid.*
[162] *Ibid.*
[163] *Ibid.*
[164] *Ibid.*
[165] "PRC: 2004 White Paper on National Defense Published," *op. cit.*, note 155.
[166] Wooton, *op. cit.*, note 149, p. 14.
[167] *Ibid.*, pp. 14-15.
[168] Swaine and Tellis, *op. cit.*, note 144.
[169] B. Raman, "National Security Mechanism," SAAG Paper No. 1228, 24 January 2005, http://www.saag.org/papers13/paper1228.html.
[170] *Ibid.*
[171] *Ibid.*
[172] I.H. Daalder and I.M. Destler, "A New NSC for a New Administration," Policy Brief No. 86, Brookings Institution, November 2000, http://www.brookings.edu/comm/policybriefs/pb68.htm.
[173] Raman, *op. cit.,* note 169.
[174] *Ibid.*
[175] A.G. Whittaker, F.C. Smith and E. McKune, "The National Security Policy Process: The National Security Council and Interagency System," Research Report, August 2005 Annual Update, Industrial College of the Armed Forces, National Defense University, US Department of Defense, accessed on 20 February, 2007, http://www.ndu.edu/icaf/, p. 6.
[176] *Ibid.*
[177] *Ibid.*
[178] *Ibid.*, p. 7.
[179] *Ibid.*, pp. 9-10
[180] *Ibid.*
[181] *Ibid.*, p. 18.
[182] *Ibid.*, p. 11.
[183] *Ibid.*, p. 12.
[184] *Ibid.*
[185] *Ibid.*, p. 10
[186] *Ibid.*, pp. 12-13.
[187] *Ibid.*, p. 13.
[188] Raman, *op. cit.,* note 169.
[189] Daalder and Destler, *op. cit.,* note 172.
[190] *Ibid.*
[191] "Road Map for National Security: Imperative for Change," The United States Commission on National Security/21st Century, Phase III Report, 31 January 2001, http://govinfo.library.unt.edu/nssg/PhaseIIIFR.pdf, p. 51.
[192] Whittaker, *et al.*, *op. cit.*, note 175, p. 45.

[193] *Ibid.*, pp. 45-46.
[194] *Ibid.*, p. 45.
[195] Raman, *op. cit.,* note 169.
[196] H.A. Rizvi, "National Security Council: A Comparative Study of Pakistan and Other Selected Countries," Pildat Background Paper, August 2005, http://fes.org.pk/publications/969-558-015-7.pdf, p. 9.
[197] *Ibid.*
[198] *Ibid.*, p. 7.
[199] *Ibid.*, p. 18.
[200] *Ibid.*, p. 9.
[201] Y. Akdogan, "A Civilian Secretary-General," Turkish Press Review, Hellenic Resources Network (HR-NET), 19 August 2004, http://www.hri.org/news/turkey/trkpr/2004/04-08-19.trkpr.html#08.
[202] Rizvi, *op. cit.*, note 196, p. 17.
[203] Raman, *op. cit.,* note 169.
[204] Rizvi, *op. cit.*, note 196, p. 17.
[205] Raman, *op. cit.,* note 169.
[206] Rizvi, *op. cit.*, note 196, p. 12.
[207] Raman, *op. cit.,* note 169.
[208] Rizvi, *op. cit.*, note 196, p. 12.
[209] *Ibid.*, p. 9
[210] *Ibid.*
[211] *Ibid.*, p. 19.
[212] "The Security Council," President of Russia, accessed on 4 June 2007, http://www.kremlin.ru/eng/articles/institut04.shtml.
[213] Raman, *op. cit.,* note 169.
[214] *Ibid.*
[215] *Ibid.*
[216] *Ibid.*
[217] Dame P. Neville-Jones, "Security Issues: Interim Position Paper," Conservative Party's National and International Security Policy Review, December 2006, http://www.conservatives.com/pdf/interimsecurityissues.pdf, p. 14.
[218] "Britain's Brown to lead new security council," The Associated Press, 3 July 2007, http://www.baltimoresun.com/news/nationworld/bal-council0703,0,4447377.story?track=rss.
[219] *Ibid.*
[220] "Brown sets out reform proposals," BBC News, 3 July 2007, http://news.bbc.co.uk/1/hi/uk_politics/6258794.stm.
[221] "Directorate general for policy and security," Ministere des affaires etrangers, Republique de France, accessed on 23 May 2007, http://www.diplomatie.gouv.fr/en/ministry_158/structure-of-the-central-administration_2051/directorate-general-for-policy-and-security_1574.html.
[222] *Ibid.*
[223] *Ibid.*
[224] *Ibid.*
[225] *Ibid.*
[226] *Ibid.*
[227] *Ibid.*

[228] M. Perelman, "How the French Fight Terror," *Foreign Policy* (Web Exclusive), January 2006, www.foreignpolicy.com/story/files/story3353.php.
[229] *Ibid.*
[230] *Ibid.*
[231] "French president urges new thinking on national security," China View, 1 August 2007, http://news.xinhuanet.com/english/2007-08/01/content_6458150.htm.
[232] "Fact Sheets," Arms Control Association, 2001, http://www.armscontrol.org/factsheets/statefct.asp.
[233] S. Xiangli, "Analysis of China's Nuclear Strategy," World Security Institute, accessed on 11 June 2007, http://www.wsichina.org/back1_05.html.
[234] H. Born, "National Governance of Nuclear Weapons: Opportunities and Constraints," *SIPRI Yearbook 2006: Armaments, Disarmament and International Security* (Oxford: Oxford University Press, 2006), p. 227.
[235] *Ibid.*, pp. 227-228.
[236] *Ibid.*, p. 228.
[237] *Ibid.*, p. 229.
[238] *Ibid.*, p. 230.
[239] *Ibid.*, p. 231.
[240] *Ibid.*
[241] *Ibid.*, pp. 231-232.
[242] *Ibid.*, p. 233.
[243] *Ibid.*
[244] *Ibid.*, p. 234.
[245] *Ibid.*
[246] *Ibid.*
[247] *Ibid.*, p. 235.
[248] *Ibid.*, p. 236.
[249] *Ibid.*
[250] *Ibid.*, p. 236-237.
[251] *Ibid.*, p. 237.
[252] *Ibid.*
[253] *Ibid.*
[254] G. Perkovich, "Faulty Promises: The US, India Nuclear Deal," *Policy Outlook* No. 21, Carnegie Endowment for International Peace, September 2005, http://www.carnegieendowment.org/publications/index.cfm?fa=view&id=17419.
[255] *Ibid.*
[256] Born, *op. cit.,* note 234, p. 238.
[257] *Ibid.*
[258] Snow, *op. cit.,* note 2, p. 24.
[259] J. Kirshner, "Globalization, Power and Prospect," in J. Kirshner (ed.), *Globalization and National Security* (New York: Routledge, 2006), p. 328.
[260] *Ibid.*, p. 337.
[261] *Ibid.*
[262] *Ibid.*
[263] *Ibid.*, pp. 337-338.
[264] *Ibid.*, p. 328.
[265] S.G. Brooks, *Producing Security* (Princeton, NJ: Princeton University Press, 2005), p. 3.
[266] *Ibid.*, p. 11.

[267] *Ibid.*, p. 6.
[268] *Ibid.*
[269] *Ibid.*
[270] *Ibid.*, p. 14.
[271] A. Lake, "Confronting Backlash States," *Foreign Affairs*, Vol. 73, No. 2, March/April 1994.
[272] B.I. Finel, B.D. Finlay and J.E. Nolan, "The Perils of Nuclear, Biological, and Chemical Weapons," in M.E. Brown (ed.), *Grave New World: Security Challenges in the 21st Century* (Washington, DC: Georgetown University Press, 2003), p. 41.
[273] *Ibid.*
[274] *Ibid.*
[275] Snow, *op. cit.,* note 2, p. 265.
[276] *Ibid.*, p. 267.
[277] *Ibid.*
[278] *Ibid.*, p. 268.
[279] *Ibid.*
[280] *Ibid.*
[281] *Ibid.*
[282] *Ibid.*
[283] *Ibid.,* p. 267.
[284] *Ibid.*, p. 269.
[285] *Ibid.,* p. 270.
[286] J.R. McNeill, "Environmental Change and Security," in Brown (ed.), *op. cit*., note 272, p. 193.
[287] *Ibid.*
[288] *Ibid.,* pp. 193-194.
[289] *Ibid.*, p. 194.
[290] C.B. Keely, "Demographic Developments and Security," in Brown (ed.), *op. cit*., note 272, p. 199.
[291] *Ibid.,* p. 200.
[292] *Ibid.*
[293] *Ibid.*
[294] *Ibid.*, p. 201.
[295] *Ibid.*
[296] *Ibid.*
[297] C. Koppell with A. Sharma, "Preventing the Next Wave of Conflict: Understanding Non-Traditional Threats to Global Stability," Report of the Non-Traditional Threats Working Group, Conflict Prevention Project, Woodrow Wilson International Center for Scholars, Washington, DC, 2003, www.wilsoncenter.org, p. 54.
[298] Keely, *op. cit*., note 290, p. 201.
[299] *Ibid.*
[300] Koppell with A. Sharma, *op. cit.,* note 297*,* p. 56.
[301] *Ibid.,* pp. 56-57.
[302] Keely, *op. cit*., note 290, p. 210.
[303] *Ibid.,* p. 211.
[304] Koppell with A. Sharma, *op. cit.,* note 297, p. 57.
[305] F.B. Adamson, "International Migration in a Globalizing World," in J. Kirshner (ed.), *op. cit*., note 259, p. 49.

[306] *Ibid.*, p. 50.
[307] *Ibid.*, p. 53.
[308] *Ibid.*, pp. 52-53.
[309] *Ibid.*, p. 53.
[310] *Ibid.*, p. 54.
[311] *Ibid.*, p. 56.
[312] I. Salehyan and K.S. Gleditsch, "Refugees and the Spread of Civil War," *International Organization* No. 60, Spring 2006, http://journals.cambridge.org/download.php?file=%2FINO%2FINO60_02%2FS0020818306060103a.pdf&code=927d90cc583f4c3479829c68c457666d, p. 343.
[313] *Ibid.*, pp. 342-343.
[314] Adamson, *op. cit.*, note 305, p. 65.
[315] "Strategic Assessment 1996: Instruments of US Power," Institute for National Strategic Studies, National Defense University, 9 July 2004, http://216.239.59.104/search?q=cache:qC3vt8of1tYJ:www.ndu.edu/inss/Strategic%2520Assessments/sa96/sa96ch01.html+%22what+makes+the+information+explosion+so%22&hl=en&ct=clnk&cd=1.
[316] Garrity, *op. cit.*, note 20, p. 119.
[317] *Ibid.*
[318] *Ibid.*, p. 121.
[319] D.E. Denning, "Information Technology and Security," in M.E. Brown (ed.), *op. cit.*, note 272, p. 91.
[320] G.L. Herrera, "New Media for a New World?" in J. Kirshner (ed.), *op. cit.*, note 259, p. 91.
[321] *Ibid.*, p. 93.
[322] Denning, *op. cit.*, note 319, p. 91.
[323] *Ibid.*
[324] *Ibid.*, p. 101.
[325] *Ibid.*, p. 103.
[326] *Ibid.*, p. 104.
[327] *Ibid.*
[328] *Ibid.*
[329] *Ibid.*
[330] N.R.F. Al-Rodhan, *The Emergence of Blogs as* a Fifth Estate *and Their Security Implications* (Genève, Éditions Slatkine, 2007).
[331] *Ibid.*, p. 58.
[332] *Ibid.*, pp. 58-59.
[333] *Ibid.*, p. 60.
[334] *Ibid.*, p. 58.
[335] D. Owen, "Transnational Mass Media Organizations and Security," in M.E. Brown, *op. cit.*, note 272, p. 236.
[336] *Ibid.*, p. 237.
[337] *Ibid.*
[338] *Ibid.*, p. 238.
[339] *Ibid.*
[340] *Ibid.*
[341] *Ibid.*, p. 240.
[342] *Ibid.*,
[343] *Ibid.*, p. 242.

[344] *Ibid.*, p. 250.
[345] Garrity, *op. cit.*, note 20, p. 121.
[346] N.R.F. Al-Rodhan, *The Five Dimensions of Global Security: Proposal for a Multi-sum Security Principle* (Berlin: LIT Verlag, 2007), p. 80.
[347] *Ibid.*, p. 82.
[348] S. Huntington, "The Clash of Civilizations?" *Foreign Affairs*, Vol. 72, No. 3, Summer 1993, http://www.foreignaffairs.org/19930601FAESSAY5188-faarticles/samuel-p-huntington/the-clash-of-civilizations.html.
[349] *Ibid.*
[350] *Ibid.*
[351] *Ibid.*
[352] N. Ferguson, "The Civilizations of the Modern World are More Likely to Collapse than Collide," 26 February 2006, http://www.telegraph.co.uk/opinion/main.jhtml?xml=/opinion/2006/02/26/do2602.xml&sSheet=/opinion/2006/02/26/ixopinion.html.
[353] *Ibid.*
[354] Kirshner, *op. cit.*, note 259, p. 336.
[355] *Ibid.*
[356] *Ibid.*
[357] H. Koechler, "The Dialogue of Civilizations: Philosophical Basis, Political Dimensions and the Relevance of International Sporting Events," paper presented at the World Cup Roundtable on Promoting Understanding among Culture and Peoples, organized by the Asia-Europe Foundation and the Korean National Commission for UNESCO, Seoul, 1 June 2002, p. 7.
[358] Al-Rodhan, *The Five Dimensions of Global Security, op. cit.,* note 346, p. 84.
[359] Garrity, *op. cit.*, note 20, p. 101.
[360] Persaud, *op. cit.*, note 12, pp. 2-3.
[361] N.R.F. Al-Rodhan, *Symbiotic Realism: A Theory of International Relations in an Instant and an Interdependent World* (Berlin: LIT Verlag, 2007), p. 81.
[362] Persaud, *op. cit.*, note 12, p. 3.
[363] Garrity, *op. cit.*, note 20, p. 108.
[364] *Ibid.*
[365] Ferraro, *op. cit.*, note 10, p. 16.
[366] *Ibid.*
[367] *Ibid.*
[368] *Ibid.*
[369] J.D. Sachs, "The Strategic Significance of Global Inequality," ECSP Report, No. 9, 2003, p. 27.
[370] *Ibid.*, p. 28.
[371] T.W. O'Donnell, "Energy and the Environment: Global Oil to 2030, A Quantitative Assessment in the Context of International Affairs," International Relations and Security Network (ISN), 2007, p. 5.
[372] R. Heinberg, "How to avoid wars, terrorism, and economic collapse," *Energy Bulletin*, 1 August 2005, http://www.energybulletin.net/7552.html.
[373] *Ibid.*
[374] O'Donnell, *op. cit.*, note 371, p. 9.
[375] *Ibid.*
[376] *Ibid.*
[377] *Ibid.*
[378] M. Harris, "Energy and Security," in M.E. Brown (ed.), *op. cit.*, note 272, p. 165.

[379] *Ibid.*
[380] N.R.F. Al-Rodhan and S. Kuepfer, *Stability of States: The Nexus Between Transnational Threats, Globalization, and Internal Resilience* (Genève, Éditions Slatkine, 2007), p. 68.
[381] *Ibid.*
[382] R. Godson, "Transnational Crime, Corruption, and Security," in M.E. Brown, *op. cit.*, note 272, p. 262.
[383] *Ibid.,* p. 264.
[384] M. Levitsky, "Transnational Criminal Networks and International Security," *Public Management*, Electronic Journal No. 2, 22 October 2003, http://e-journal.spa.msu.ru/images/File/2003/levitsky(1).pdf, p. 1.
[385] T.S. Thomas and S.D. Kiser, "Lords of the Silk Route: Violent Non-State Actors in Central Asia," INSS Occasional Paper No. 43, Institute for National Security Studies, May 2002, www.usafa.af.mil/inss, p. 34.
[386] P-A. Chouvy and L. Laniel, "Drug Production and State Stability," December 2006, www.ceri-sciencespo.com/archive/sept06/rapport_ceri_sgdn.pdf.
[387] Levitsky, *op. cit.*, note 384, p. 3.
[388] *Ibid.*, p. 2.
[389] "What is Human Trafficking?" HumanTrafficking.com, The Research and Training Center of Polaris Project, accessed on 19 March, 2006, http://www.polarisproject.org/humantrafficking/trafficking_ht3/what_is_ht.htm.
[390] *Ibid.*
[391] S. Kupfer, "The New Slavery: The dark underside of globalization," *The Ripon Forum* (Spring 2004), p. 9.
[392] Snow, *op. cit.,* note 2, p. 250.
[393] *Ibid.,* p. 251.
[394] M. van Creveld, *The Transformation of War* (New York: Free Press, 1991), p. 197.
[395] Snow, *op. cit.,* note 2, p. 263.
[396] *Ibid.,* p. 274.
[397] A.K. Cronin, "Transnational Terrorism and Security," in M.E. Brown (ed.), *op. cit.*, note 272, p. 288.
[398] K.P. Mueller, "The Paradox of Liberal Hegemony," in J. Kirshner (ed.), *op. cit.*, note 259, p. 155.
[399] Cronin, *op. cit.*, note 397, p. 288.
[400] *Ibid.,* p. 296.
[401] *Ibid.,* p. 297.
[402] *Ibid.*
[403] Finel, *et al., op. cit.*, note 272, p. 41.
[404] *Ibid.*
[405] *Ibid.*
[406] *Ibid.*, p. 39.
[407] *Ibid.*
[408] *Ibid.*, p. 40.
[409] *Ibid.*, p. 39.
[410] Garrity, *op. cit.*, note 20, p. 110
[411] *Ibid.*
[412] *Ibid.*, p. 111.
[413] *Ibid.*
[414] Finel, *et al., op. cit.*, note 272, p. 54.

[415] Garrity, *op. cit.*, note 20, p. 110.
[416] Finel, *et al.*, *op. cit.*, note 272, p. 56.
[417] *Ibid.*, pp. 54-55.
[418] *Ibid.*, p. 55.
[419] *Ibid.*, p. 56.
[420] J.L. Husbands, "The Proliferation of Conventional Weapons and Technologies," in M.E. Brown (ed.), *op. cit.*, note 272, p. 65.
[421] Levitsky, *op. cit.*, note 384, p. 2.
[422] Husbands, *op. cit.*, note 420, p. 70.
[423] *Ibid.*
[424] D. Avant, "The Marketization of Security," in J. Kirshner (ed.), *op. cit.*, note 259, pp. 107-108.
[425] C. Holmqvist, "Private Security Companies: The Case for Regulation," SIPRI Policy Paper No. 9, Stockholm International Peace Research Institute (SIPRI), January 2005, http://books.sipri.org/product_info?c_product_id=191, p. 23.
[426] *Ibid.*, p. 15.
[427] Avant, *op. cit.*, note 424, p. 117.
[428] *Ibid.*, p. 123.
[429] G. Cecchine and M. Moore, "Infectious Disease and National Security: Strategic Information Needs," Rand National Defense Research Institute, 2006, http://192.5.14.110/pubs/technical_reports/2006/RAND_TR405.pdf, p. xiii.
[430] *Ibid.*, p. 1.
[431] *Ibid.*
[432] *Ibid.*, p. 7.
[433] *Ibid.*
[434] *Ibid.*
[435] *Ibid.*, p. 8.
[436] *Ibid.*, p. 5.
[437] *Ibid.*
[438] *Ibid.*, p. 17.
[439] *Ibid.*
[440] B. Boxer, "Providing Basic Human Security," *The Washington Quarterly,* Vol. 26, No. 2, Spring 2003, http://www.twq.com/03spring/docs/03spring_boxer.pdf, p. 203.
[441] Cecchine and Moore, *op. cit.*, note 429, p. 18.
[442] *Ibid.*
[443] P.W. Singer, "AIDS and International Security," *Survival,* Vol. 44, No. 1, p. 148.
[444] Cecchine and Moore, *op. cit.*, note 429, p. 17.
[445] *Ibid.*, p. xiv.
[446] S.E. Rice, "Strengthening Weak States: A 21st Century Imperative," paper prepared for a conference sponsored by the Security and Peace Initiative, 6 June 2006, www.securitypeace.org.
[447] N.R.F. Al-Rodhan, *The Five Dimensions of Global Security, op. cit.*, note 346, p. 49.
[448] *Ibid.*
[449] *Ibid.,* pp. 50-51.
[450] *Britannica Concise Encyclopedia*, Answers.com, accessed on 8 May 2007, http://www.answers.com/topic/global-warming, s.v. "Global Warming."

451 "Climate Change 2007: Climate Change Impacts, Adaptation and Vulnerability," Working Group II Contribution to the Intergovernmental Panel on Climate Change, Fourth Assessment Report, Summary for Policymakers, 6 April 2007, http://downloads.heartland.org/20904.pdf.
452 *Ibid.*, p. 10.
453 "National Security and the Threat of Climate Change," CAN Corporation, 16 April 2007, http://www.securityandclimate.cna.org/report/National%20Security%20and%20the%20Threat%20of%20Climate%20Change.pdf.
454 "Climate Change 2007: Climate Change Impacts, Adaptation and Vulnerability," *op. cit.*, note 451, p. 10.
455 "Climate Change Poses Serious Threat to US National Security," *Energy Bulletin*, 17 April 2007, http://www.energybulletin.net/28744.html.
456 Garrity, *op. cit.*, note 20, p. 117.
457 Koppell with A. Sharma, *op. cit.,* note 297, p. 81.
458 *Ibid.,* p. 73.
459 *Ibid.,* p. 74.
460 Garrity, *op. cit.*, note 20, p. 116.
461 McNeill, *op. cit.*, note 286, p. 191.
462 Garrity, *op. cit.*, note 20, p. 118.
463 *Ibid.*
464 Koppell with A. Sharma, *op. cit.,* note 297, pp. 72-73.
465 McNeill, *op. cit.*, note 286, p. 191.
466 *Ibid.*
467 *Ibid.*, p. 192.
468 *Ibid.*, p. 191.
469 Koppell with A. Sharma, *op. cit.,* note 297, p. 2.
470 M.E. Brown, "Security Problems and Security Policy in a Grave New World," in Brown (ed.), *op. cit.*, note 272, p. 312.
471 *Ibid.*
472 Al-Rodhan, *The Five Dimensions of Global Security, op. cit.,* note 346; Al-Rodhan, *Symbiotic Realism, op. cit.,* note 361; N.R.F. Al-Rodhan, *Transcivilizational Synergy* (working title), *forthcoming,* 2008.
473 Al-Rodhan, *The Five Dimensions of Global Security, op. cit.,* note 347.
474 M. Mihalka, "Cooperative Security in the 21st Century," *Connections: The Quarterly Journal*, Vol. 4, No. 4, Winter 2005, p. 114.
475 H. Haenggi, "Making Sense of Security Sector Governance," accessed on 5 July 2007, se2.isn.ch/serviceengine/FileContent?serviceID=21&fileid=58E64B8B-488C-F952-40DC-BA7C13BD4393&lng=en, p. 5.
476 L. Axworthy, "Human Security and Global Governance: Putting People First," *Global Governance*, No. 7, 2001, p. 19.
477 Al-Rodhan, *The Five Dimensions of Global Security, op. cit.,* note 346.
478 B. Buzan, O. Weaver and J. de Wilde, *Security: A New Framework for Analysis* (Boulder, Co., London: Lynne Rienner, 1998), pp. 22-23, 123.
479 Al-Rodhan, *The Five Dimensions of Global Security, op. cit.,* note 346, p. 13.
480 *Ibid.*
481 *Ibid.*
482 *Ibid.,* p. 97.
483 *Ibid.,* p. 105.
484 *Ibid.*

[485] *Ibid.,* pp. 15-16.
[486] *Ibid.,* p. 31.
[487] *Ibid.,* p. 107.
[488] *Ibid.*, p. 108.
[489] *Ibid.*, p. 109.
[490] *Ibid.*
[491] *Ibid.*, pp. 110-111.
[492] *Ibid.*, p. 112.
[493] *Ibid.*, p. 113-114.
[494] Al-Rodhan, *Symbiotic Realism op. cit.,* note 361.
[495] Brown, *op. cit.,* note 470, p. 306.
[496] *Ibid.*
[497] *Ibid.,* p. 307.
[498] Al-Rodhan, *Symbiotic Realism, op. cit.,* note 361, p. 11.
[499] *Ibid.,* p. 12.
[500] *Ibid.,* p. 13.
[501] *Ibid.,* p. 14.
[502] *Ibid.,* p. 104.
[503] *Ibid.,* p. 138.
[504] *Ibid.,* p. 100.
[505] *Ibid.,* p. 10.
[506] *Ibid.,* p. 14.
[507] *Ibid.,* p. 15.
[508] *Ibid.,* p. 132.
[509] *Ibid.,* p. 117.
[510] *Ibid.,* p. 15.
[511] *Ibid.,* pp. 135-136.
[512] N.R.F. Al-Rodhan, *Transcivilizational Synergy*, *op. cit.,* note 472.
[513] N.R.F. Al-Rodhan and L. Watanabe, *A Proposal for* Inclusive *Peace and Security* (Genève, Éditions Slatkine, 2007), pp. 98-99.
[514] *Ibid.,* p. 99.
[515] *Ibid.*
[516] *Ibid.,* p. 91.
[517] *Ibid.,* p. 101.
[518] *Ibid.,* p. 102.
[519] G.J. Ikenberry and Anne-Marie Slaughter, "Forging a World of Liberty under Law: US National Security in the 21st Century," The Princeton Project Papers, The Woodrow Wilson School of Public and International Affairs, Princeton University, 27 September 2006.
[520] *Ibid.,* pp. 17-18.
[521] D.M. Gerstein, *Securing America's Future: National Strategy in the Information Age* (Westport, Ct.: Praeger Security International, 2005), p. 134.
[522] *Ibid.,* p. 135.
[523] *Ibid.*
[524] *Ibid.,* p. 137.
[525] "Road Map for National Security: Addendum on Structure and Process Analyses," US Commission on National Security/21st Century, Vol. 1, 15 April 2001, http://govinfo.library.unt.edu/nssg/addedum/Vol_I.pdf, p. 17.

[526] N.R.F. Al-Rodhan, *The Emergence of Blogs as* a Fifth Estate *and Their Security Implications, op. cit.,* note 330, p. 63.
[527] E. Dowdeswell, P.A. Singer and A.S. Daar, "Increasing Human Security Through Biotechnology," *International Journal of Biotechnology*, Vol. 8, Nos. 1-2, 9 February 2006, Inderscience Enterprises Ltd., http://www.ingentaconnect.com/content/ind/ijbt/2006/00000008/F0020001/art00008, p. 124.
[528] *Ibid.,* p. 122.
[529] P. Lin and B. Wang, "Nanotechnology in Global Security and Economics," *Genetic Engineering and Biotechnology News*, 1 May 2006, http://www.genengnews.com/articles/chitem.aspx?aid=1574&chid=0.
[530] Dowdeswell, *et al.*, *op. cit.*, note 527, p. 129.
[531] Lin and Wang, *op. cit.*, note 529.
[532] Dowdeswell, *et al.*, *op. cit.*, note 527, p. 127.
[533] *Ibid.,* p. 126.
[534] J. Brada, A.M. Kutan and T.M. Yigit, "The Effects of Transition and Political Instability on Foreign Direct Investment in ECE Emerging Markets," 2005, www.unece.org/ead/sem/sem2005/papers/FDIUNECE1.pdf.
[535] J. Bray, *et al.*, "Investing in Stability," Report by the United Nations Environment Programme and International Institute for Sustainable Development, 2004, http://www.unepfi.org/fileadmin/documents/investing_in_stability_final_report_2004.pdf, p. 13.
[536] Al-Rodhan, *Symbiotic Realism, op. cit.,* note 361.
[537] Gerstein, *op. cit.*, note 521, p. 138.
[538] *Ibid.*
[539] "Executive Summary," in *Mapping the Global Future*, Report of the National Intelligence Council's 2020 Project, December 2004, http://www.dni.gov/nic/NIC_globaltrend2020_es.html.
[540] *Ibid.*
[541] Gerstein, *op. cit.*, note 521, p. 144.
[542] *Ibid.*
[543] *Ibid.*, p. 156.
[544] *Ibid.*.
[545] N.R.F. Al-Rodhan, *The Role of Education in Global Security* (Genève, Éditions Slatkine, 2007), pp. 105-106.
[546] *Mapping the Global Future*, *op. cit.*, note 539.
[547] *Ibid.*
[548] *Ibid.*
[549] "Pervasive Insecurity," in *Mapping the Global Future*, Report of the National Intelligence Council's 2020 Project, December 2004, http://www.dni.gov/nic/NIC_globaltrend2020_s4.html#scen.
[550] "Conflict Analysis," The World Bank, 2007, http://web.worldbank.org/WBSITE/EXTERNAL/TOPICS/EXTSOCIALDEVELOPMENT/EXTCPR/0,,contentMDK:20486708~menuPK:1260893~pagePK:148956~piPK:216618~theSitePK:407740,00.html.
[551] "Human Rights of Women," United Nations Fourth World Conference on Women, Beijing, September 1995, http://www.un.org/womenwatch/daw/beijing/platform/human.htm#diagnosis.
[552] *Ibid.*

[553] "Who's On First? Decision-Making in the Midst of Disaster," Leadership and Change, W.P. Carey School, Arizona State University, 28 September 2005, http://knowledge.wpcarey.asu.edu/index.cfm?fa=viewfeature&id=1111.
[554] *Ibid.*
[555] "Religion and American Foreign Policy: Prophetic, Perilous, Inevitable," Event Transcript, The Pew Forum on Religion and Public Life, 5 February 2003, http://pewforum.org/events/?EventID=40.
[556] *Ibid.*
[557] *Ibid.*
[558] T. Barry, *et al.*, "A Global Good Neighbor Ethic for International Relations" (Second Edition), International Relations Center and Foreign Policy in Focus, 12 December 2006, http://ggn.irc-online.org/neighbor/142, p. 7.
[559] "Road Map for National Security: Addendum on Structure and Process Analyses," *op. cit.*, note 525, p. 18.
[560] Al-Rodhan, *The Five Dimensions of Global Security, op. cit.,* note 346.
[561] Al-Rodhan, *Symbiotic Realism, op. cit.,* note 361.
[562] Al-Rodhan, *Transcivilizational Synergy, op. cit.,* note 472.

INDEX

M

N

O

P